HOLY HOT VISIBILITY

Shine Brighter with Less Fear

7 Gateways to Activate Prosperity, Step Out in Confidence,
and Become the Soul-Led Luminary You Are Here To Be

LUCINDA RAE

Praises for
Holy Hot Visibility

"*Holy Hot Visibility* is a sacred journey of self-discovery. Lucinda Rae's words are a balm for the soul, touching the deepest parts of your being. She leads you through the labyrinth of fear and self-doubt with grace and wisdom, showing you the way to your true self. This book is not just a read; it's a transformational experience that will ignite your inner light and empower you to shine brightly in the world."

— *Sunny Dawn Johnston, Author, Speaker and Psychic Medium*

"In a world that often makes women feel like they're 'too much,' *Holy Hot Visibility* is a courageous call to action to overcome these limiting beliefs and to step into their power boldly. Any female entrepreneur looking to build confidence, influence, impact, and a robust online presence will love Lucinda's raw vulnerability and sage guidance. I especially enjoyed how she blends spiritual insights with authentic branding guidance. Bravo!"

— *Crystal Andrus Morissette, Best-Selling Author of Six Books, Featured on Oprah*

"As a former *CoverGirl* Super Model, I've spent some of my career in the spotlight. Yet, *Holy Hot Visibility* by Lucinda Rae has been a revelation, helping me to see where I have still been hiding and holding back. It has reignited my deep desire to boldly share my heart, voice and gifts with humanity and I now have these wise words, meditations and practical steps to come back to over and over again whenever my fears and tendency to hide creep back in. This book is like having your very own visibility coach in the palm of your hands!

Lucinda's wisdom transcends the world of glamour and lights. Her words touch my soul and deepen my awareness that true visibility isn't just about what the world sees on the outside, but the radiant essence we carry within and vulnerably share. This book has reminded me that authentic and courageous expression of my true essence is the most captivating beauty of all. My visibility journey feels more aligned, easeful and purposeful since reading this soulful and practical guide book. Thank you, Lucinda, for illuminating this visibility path for us!"

— *Renee Jeffus, Former CoverGirl Super Model,*
Revolutionary Radiance Mentor

For permissions requests, please contact:
Lucinda Rae | email: Lucinda@HelloLucinda.com

This book is intended to provide information and guidance to its readers and is sold with the understanding that the author and publisher are not engaged in rendering professional advice or services. If expert assistance or counseling is needed, the services of a professional should be sought.

Cover design: Lucinda Rae
Cover photo: Onyay Pheori
Layout design: by Lucinda Rae

Learn more online at:
www.HelloLucinda.com

ISBN 978-1-7344034-2-8
10 9 8 7 6 5 4 3 2 1

To the women of the past, present, and future,
who boldly shine their light, dare to be seen,
and share their voices,
I honor your courage amidst adversity.

In the depths of history, your brilliance defied narrow
perceptions. Mistakenly misjudged, your spirits remained
resilient,
your creativity unwavering.

This book is a heartfelt tribute to your enduring legacy,
guiding creative entrepreneurs on their journeys.

May your misunderstood essence inspire authenticity
and healing in others and in life.

May this book be your support and a reminder
to persist as brilliantly authentic selves,
for that's what our world desperately needs.

In your radiant presence, we find courage,
and in your stories,
the strength of visibility.

TABLE OF CONTENTS

BONUS GIFT

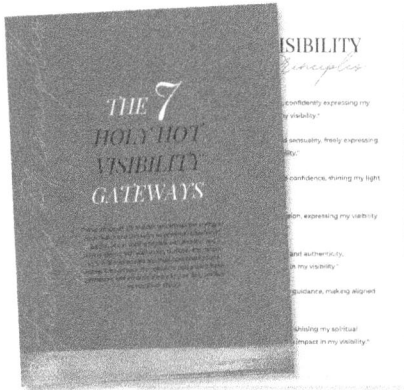

DOWNLOAD YOUR FREE

THE 7 HOLY HOT VISIBILITY GATEWAYS

Combined affirmations to support your shining brighter with less fear and staying aligned to your vision, purpose and mission. Integrate these into your daily practice for maximum impact.

Download it here:
www.hellolucinda.com/freegift

HOW THIS BOOK WORKS

What and Why Holy?

We traverse the HOLY – the currency of life itself that flows through you in every moment of our lives as we are held in wholeness with the Divine. It is the creative essence that brings us alive and we cling to during the storms the world brings us. Holy is the sunlight that streams through our being to remind us that we have everything within us to know and embody heaven on Earth.

Holy is who you are at your core as you are creating your life, your journey into wealth, and as you are sharing your gifts and true voice with the world.

Holy is also the stillness we can reside in when in the deep bliss of meditation, prayer, breathwork, and other ceremonial rituals to connect to realms unseen. It is these internal realms that sensitive souls and introverts crave and seek to recharge, and the temple of silence within, where we seek the eternal Great Mystery our soul longs to merge with.

Holy is the internal realm of the mystic within that we desire to tap into. It is also the place where we feel safe to crawl up in the Invisibility Cave to transcend this world, this body, this ego to dissolve into the oneness we desire.

Holy, for the many spirit-centered clients for whom I have designed websites, graphics, and done personal brand photo-shoots, is their work as their life purpose, or calling.

So, if you're hiding out, you're likely not sharing your gifts in the way you're meant to.

As I have discovered over the years, hiding out can often be a coping mechanism for highly sensitives and empathic types. That's why part of my purpose is to bring more awareness to this aspect of using meditation and spirituality as unconscious escapism and illuminate the spaces and places where this happens.

Why? Because embodiment is where it's at with Holy Hot Visibility. Our bodies and businesses become the bridge, bringing our soulful calling, our unique medicine, and gifts to the world.

You can't do that unless you are embodied in your visibility and leadership. Otherwise, we spin in some other dimension, flailing with insecurities, confusion, or overwhelm and potentially miss the boat of bringing that dream that lives inside of us to others. You must become the practitioner of your soul's language as you bring your heaven-to-Earth sauce into this descended sphere. That is why we must learn how to hold sacred this HOLY within us and integrate it with the HOT of our purpose.

What and Why Hot?

When we step into HOT, we marry the soulful with the embodiment; we take the journey of feeling good in our skin no matter what is on our skin. Yes, this can be your womanly curves or that sparkle in your eye.

Your soul is the reason you're on fire to share what you love to do and make good money; it's that thing I call your Prosperous Why. We'll get into the concept of your Prosperous Why more later in the book, but for now know that your Prosperous Why is that fire beneath your feet and the sun to wear as your crown as you shine like the blazing molten flame of the life only you are here to live. To be and express that creative lifeforce in the world in only a way that you can do.

This is the essence of HOTNESS.

These two pillars are the cornerstones of the work of getting visible in the world: Holy and Hot... divinity and passion... glamour meets God. The intermingled inner masculine and feminine and back again; your prayers, meditations, your feeling of significance, and your "*oh heck, yes!*"

You are ALL of it. You are the integration – the alchemy of holy-hot. I used to think of them in terms of duality; however, as I have walked the path I realized it is essential to embody the Divine and embrace our physicality. We are the emergence of the fire that sears through our being and the divinity that flows through it all.

Imagine most of the world getting up drearily to their alarm clock, unenthusiastically having their morning cuppa to try and wake themselves up enough to get in the car and drive to their day job. They go through the routines, endeavor to cordially greet their co-workers, endeavor to live up to their bosses' expectations, and do this day in and day out, hanging on until the weekend. Before they know it, if they are able – and blessed enough – they are planning to enter retirement to have a few years to enjoy "the good life."

What if instead you were leaping out of bed with bells on to make your difference in the world?

Maybe your journey is the road of philanthropy and donating time, resources, or expertise to charitable causes and helping those in need?

Or seeking inner peace through spirituality and mindfulness?

Maybe it's to be the best stay-at-home mama you can be?

And since this book was written for spiritual creative entrepreneurs and soulfully sensitive dreamers, you might be a parent who also has a passion to empower young girls, or to light the fire under others to stoke their best selves, or share your unique light through your art to inspire others and uplift their souls.

Perhaps you are a writing coach who helps others get their personal life stories written while you are working on your life's greatest work – your own inspirational memoir. You could be a business coach that blazes the paths for women to step into their wealth or create an iconic brand that sizzles in riches.

Whatever it is, when you pair the HOLY with the HOT, you come to know the most fulfilling expansive blessings united with anything you do. For those who are living a life attuned with the Divine, you have a purpose in all you do.

As you cultivate this, we can align with what brings you the most joy while ensuring financial stability, and ideally, flourishing into even greater abundance.

What and Why Visibility?

You have embodied your soul and the innate confidence and magnetism of being a woman; your next step is taking all of the holy and all of the living, scintillating HOT and bringing it out into the world.

It brings up the skeletons in the closet, the daggers in our egos, and the basic stuff we can work on. Those very things that try to stop us from being visible.

We get to relearn to release old fears or self-sabotage and boost our confidence and self-worth in new ways each time we walk through a new door of visibility. In a sense, it crafts us anew as we alchemize in the crucible of visibility and the never-ending layers of growth it takes us on.

Because the world, and the people who are meant to be mentored, inspired, and led by you, are waiting... and how are they going to find you if you're not shining from the inside and out?

This is about putting out your "bat signal" so they can find you – to be the beacon and the lighthouse to share your authentic and one-and-only medicine. And doing it again and again so we can be there for our audience, ourselves, and our purpose and legacy we desire to share and allow to continue to ripple out beyond ourselves.

How You Can Use This Book

In the following pages, I present the 7 Gateways, which follow the structure of the chakras, as a transformative journey towards gaining greater awareness of the patterns and shadowy aspects that may impact your experience of visibility. Throughout the book I use examples from my own life in the hopes of providing narratives that resonate with you, allowing you to recall moments from your past that might have triggered limiting beliefs, hindering your desire to be seen.

At the conclusion of each Gateway chapter, you will find a section titled "Your Path Through the Gateway." Here, I weave together the emotional, spiritual, and psychological facets of healing within the energy centers, facilitating a transition toward practical application in the real world. This section prompts you to consider how these insights can be integrated into your personal brand or purposeful calling, enabling you to keep going on the journey of bringing your authentic self into the world.

To further support you in progressing through the seven gateways and manifesting your vision as a creative spiritual entrepreneur, I have also included "Gateway Journal Prompts." These prompts serve as a valuable tool, encouraging you to explore and solidify your next steps based on the teaching of the gateway. By actively engaging with these exercises, you can transform your aspirations into tangible reality as you build your business and discover your unique pathway.

I feel big gratitude for your joining me in the journey of Holy Hot Visibility. Together, we are redefining what it means to be seen and celebrated as our essential and authentic selves.

Why Now?

In the era of the increasing path of the creative spiritual entrepreneur, the world needs someone who understands critical thinking and is focusing their life to create impact for the greater good. Some might say the world has been led by the patriarchal leader, doing it for ego, greed, and power.

I want to see the healer, highly sensitive, empathic, and often introverted magical types be seen and heard in a way that works for them.

The willingness to be audaciously seen is a challenge for most entrepreneurs... and can especially be an ongoing growth edge and initiation especially for introverts, soul empaths and highly sensitives.

Becoming seen and heard is the cream of the crop in online business success, so how do we put ourselves out there and feel good about it?

I have a few things I've learned over the years as I've mentored my creative spiritual entrepreneur clients on how to activate the natural strengths in ways that align with them.

What if I told you keeping all that depth and wisdom on the inside is robbing your light from those who most need it?

One day I realized not all entrepreneurs take on the rock star persona, waving their hands wildly at the camera and standing on tables yelling at the audience to stand out.

The secret golden nugget to remember is, visibility does not mean "all eyes on you, babe."

It's a beautiful, subtle reframe about sharing your brilliance, ideas, and expertise in a way that is genuine and authentic. That's why I've encouraged "authentic visibility" for years in my messaging.

You don't need to holler the loudest to make a purposeful, meaningful change in the world.

And yes, even with that hesitancy to stand up and stand out, visibility is still essential to your thriving business.

Your clients or audience seek services that align with their values and beliefs. They want to know the people behind the service and feel the aligned and similar values.

It's been thrilling to watch the way this shines through in marketing while leading with authenticity and humanness. I started searching for the emergence of those who are their industries' "best-kept secrets" but also have a desire to share more of their light and positive impact in more expansive ways. As a branding mentor and designer, I found the pain of the most amazing women doing things so unique to them and their soul, but still playing small and not sure how to create their brand. I helped them understand they ARE the brand and that is enough! They just need to allow the personal brand to be sung from the rooftops in ways that work in alignment for them.

For these spiritual creative entrepreneurs, visibility is not duck-lipped selfies and showing off their new eyelashes. This is about deep, intimate, and authentic visibility. Being who they are and being brave enough to show up and stand in their God-given one-and-only uniqueness. It's about how, in their nakedness, as if they had just emerged from the original Garden, they were vulnerable and self-loving enough to walk past the trolls and internet haters with awareness and self-love – chin held high.

This became the spiritual and self-development work for the majority of my clients, and clearly and intrinsically tied in with their life purpose. It would also be their test, heroine's journey, and a soulful path to walk with the intention to become more and more upleveled in this path of showing up, failing forward, and knowing that done is better than perfect in their consistent accomplishment and allowing the shine from within.

Why Me?

It's true. In sitting down with my cup of chai to begin this book, I had some moments of the shady-self rush in to offer the first dance. You know, those cracks where insecurity streams in with pocketfuls of second guesses...

So I signed up for a writing "bootcamp," where I would be held accountable to get this book – the concept of which had come up over the years with many titles and angles – done, already. Well, at least I got the first few pages written.

Addendum from the final edits of this book: fours year later, it is finally ready to come into the world. Sometimes getting it done, already, has a life of its own.

As I am writing this, we've just marked the summer solstice on the calendar here in the northern hemisphere, everything is bright and shining at its full zenith. The sun shines most hours of the day and flowers are blooming and things are thriving. It's the point where the seasons reflect their most visibility. I felt called to address the seasons and aspects of our lives and businesses as entrepreneurs, what this thing called *visibility* is and the ways to activate, elevate, and sustain it in our creative businesses and lives.

And, with a deep breath, the words became one long exhale on the wind of self-inquiry, business expertise, and life story with what eventually became Hot Holy Visibility.

The idea that came in via the vehicle of the Divine intelligence within spoke loudly and clear...to share... to inspire... this:

I NEED TO BE MY OWN EXPERT.

WE ALL NEED TO BE OUR OWN EXPERTS.

Simple, right?

"What does that even mean?" questioned one voice in my head, while another challenged back: "Well, what makes ME an expert in visibility when I still hide and love my secret power of being invisible in the world?"

Ironically enough, I realized that the very thing I love about hiding is what I use to my advantage when helping my clients. And, yet, there is also the sense that if I cheer and empower other women I don't really have to do it for myself... right?

 Then the Wise ("Holy") Voice inquired:

What exactly is it that you love about hiding?

And the Sassy Fiery ("Hot") Voice challenged back:

I can hide if I feel like it. And I can be bright and shine if I want to.

Then a third voice chimed in... which appeared to be the wise and more integrated ("Visibility") Voice:

Perhaps there is a balance. You can find healthy ways to go within, and then come out so people can enjoy your unique brilliance to share.

And so the visibility story begins...

We get to create ourselves and recreate ourselves.

That is the blessing to be alive.

PRELUDE

"Our deepest fear is not that we are inadequate. Our deepest fear is that we are powerful beyond measure. It is our light, not our darkness that most frightens us. We ask ourselves, 'Who am I to be brilliant, gorgeous, talented, fabulous?'
Actually, who are you not to be? You are a child of God. Your playing small does not serve the world..."
— *Marianne Williamson*

In 2020, I was hired as an event photographer for Marianne Williamson's presidential campaign. This was surreal, to say the least. Williamson's book *Illuminata* was one of the first books that reignited the journey of prayer in my early adult years, and since then I had lightly followed her as I danced on my merry way along the spiritual path.

Now, decades later, she was running to be first woman president.

The night of the event, I looked on in amazement at the crowd, the blaring lights, and stage adorned with a giant archway of red, white, and blue balloons. A tunnel vision moment followed as I realized I was about to share that stage with her. I was aware of the perspiration in the darkness beneath my lilac double-breasted chic blazer; butterflies of hesitation fluttered around my stomach.

While all eyes would be on the star as she gave her mic-drop speech — they could also potentially be looking at me for a moment or more.

Let's just say being seen was never my thing.

Without missing a beat, the all-too-familiar demons of insecurity began hissing... from the extra weight I was carrying after giving birth to my son two months prior to the spot of baby spit-up on my black tank top that occurred moments before I left the house. Would anyone notice that my lens wasn't the typical massive event zoom lens like the safari guys use on *National Geographic* nature shows? Underlying these thoughts was the bizarre overall shame of being human and the fear that the flaws, real or imagined, only I knew about myself would be exposed.

The comedic irony of this was not lost on me. There I was, a brand mentor who over the years had encouraged and uplifted women past their nonsensical shame and insecurities, coming face to face once again with my own visibility issues. These experiences flashed through my mind, eliciting a laugh audible only to me, that transmuted the fear and allowed me to see this moment for what it truly was: an opportunity to witness myself in true vulnerability.

Most, if not all, of us can recall such experiences. Maybe there are lifetimes of layering and complex reasonings of being persecuted or punished, and maybe we just aren't feeling confident in a particular moment.

Whatever the case, the terror we feel in just being seen is raw and real.

I quickly noticed these inner voices and realized no one would be judging me in these odd ways of my own shadowy self-talk. As these ideas were transmuted, I was able to step into who I really was – a blessed soul and child of the Divine One – and focus on the task at hand.

While I wanted to walk straight up the aisle to snap some close-up power shots, I was also cognizant that this might detract attention from Marianne, which would be unprofessional. In that moment, I watched one of Marianne's assistants sneak up the aisle in a crouched position so as not to draw the audience's attention.

Keen in my timing, I waited until the crowd leaped up in a standing ovation; then, with a swift gait, I flowed with the apex of applause and merged with its energy. My shutter fluttered in ecstatic capture, getting the broad, "satisfied politician" I had been waiting for, akin to a leopard in the tree ready to leap upon its subject.

For a moment the cheering and clapping of the crowd was for me and all the work I had done to move past my visibility issues. Then my camera lowered and I admired Marianne as she received the praise for her brilliance. Flags and campaign signs waved in the air. Whistles rang out, serving as prospective votes before a single lever was pulled.

I shared in the capture, the essence, the moment, and made it real through my lens, capturing Ms. Potential President in all her glory.

It floored me to see a woman so powerfully integrated. Marianne was an example of being in her moment. She was showing up in her "hot" self on-fire on that stage, preaching passionately how we need to "heal the soul of America" and how this country needs to atone for the past. And she was being visible in her "holy" side referencing God and mentioning consciousness in her debate speeches.

I had flashes of her at a round table with leaders from all over the world coming together in prayer and meditation. What if...? In that moment, I could imagine the world peace that children all over wish for at Christmas in lieu of toys, that dream that themes dozens of songs, and that is the final resting place of religions. The World to Come. The New Age. Heaven on Earth.

And, that night, with my lens, I captured yet another woman in her zone of purpose and prosperity. I too was in my glory, doing that at which I excel at: helping others shine.

This event was a whole new ballgame for me. I had done a handful of event photoshoots before, however, my focus was primarily on personal brand portrait photography. Yet, when I heard Marianne was coming to Santa Barbara to speak for her campaign, I contacted the host of the event – something I never would have had the cojones or self-worth to do five years earlier. In taking this bold action to pitch myself, I elevated my career, my portfolio, and my visibility as a photographer. I was also invited to photograph the VIP luncheon the next day at a stunning private estate in Montecito and hear more inspired speeches, take close up photos and headshots, enjoy delicious food and mingle a bit.

Part of being visible is taking leaps. And yes, it sometimes requires faking it 'til you make it. A big part of it is having self-compassion and learning how to heal some deep programming and wounds in the collective as women around being seen in a way that works for each of us.

I had to remember to embrace myself as the worthy, Divine child that was here to bless the world with her gifts. To release the doubt that might endlessly tempt me and instead allow the Light that lights the whole world to shine through me.

And it wouldn't be the last time I would remind myself of this on the journey.

Sometimes the path is just about remembering.

And remembering again.

I have poured my soul and sweat into this journey of visibility to my clients as a business coach, personal brand photographer, and brand designer for many amazing women entrepreneurs. And I have flipped and turned and poked and assessed the one thing that almost every woman I have worked with has had to work through in some form or facet: *visibility*.

And yes, I've taken a few notes along the way, and would love to share some steps that got me to the place in my journey today...

It's time to light that torch of purpose that sets the soul on fire to accomplish our legacy.

As I write this, I raise my rose kombucha to you in hopes you may open the doorway to find your own flavor of Holy Hot Visibility as you blaze and ignite the trail of your own luminous life.

Part One
Envisioning

ROOTEDNESS & BELONGING

From Unsafe to Safe

Security, Stability, and Embodiment

"Soul work is not a high road. It's a deep fall into an unforgiving darkness that won't let you go until you find the song that sings you home."
— *McCall Erickson*

A Note on the 7 Gateways

It's amazing what the visibility journey can teach us about self-love and increased prosperity in business. It seems to never end and there are aspects at every step of the rainbow that we can look deeply into and bring forth and empower as emanations for our whole self.

You've probably heard of the chakras before; you may have also heard that the chakras are a complicated system of energy centers located throughout the body, from the base of the spine to the crown of the head.

And do you know what they are and why they matter?

Throughout the book, I'll refer to each chakra as a "gateway" when it represents its guiding principle. Each chakra is linked to unique emotional and spiritual qualities, and maintaining their balance is crucial for holistic well-being and good health. As we explore the chakras as a framework for your visibility and their impact on our lives, let's start with the basics of the seven main chakras, where healing and transformation serve as the gateway to achieving your Holy Hot Visibility.

The Root Chakra

This one is at the bottom of the spine, the root, or first chakra, is associated with our feeling of safety and security. When this chakra is balanced, we feel grounded and stable. We are able to weather life's storms with ease and grace. Red is a color related to the root chakra.

The Sacral Chakra

The sacral chakra, or second chakra, is situated just under the navel. It is associated with our creative energy and sexual expression. When this chakra is balanced, we feel pleasure and vitality. We are able to enjoy our bodies and sexuality without shame or guilt. This chakra is related with the color orange.

The Solar Plexus Chakra

Located just above the navel, the solar plexus, or third chakra is associated with our personal power and sense of identity. When this chakra is balanced, we feel confident and self-assured. We are able to stand in our truth and express ourselves authentically. Yellow is the color associated with this chakra.

The Heart Chakra

The fourth chakra which is situated in the center of the chest, is connected with love, compassion, and forgiveness. When this chakra is balanced, we feel openhearted and are able to give and receive love unconditionally. The heart chakra is associated with emerald green.

The Throat Chakra

The throat, which is situated at the base of the throat, or fifth chakra is associated with communication and self-expression. When this chakra is balanced, we feel confident in our voice and ability to communicate our truth. We are able to express ourselves clearly and confidently. Blue is a hue related to the throat chakra.

The Third-Eye Chakra

The third eye, or sixth chakra is situated between the eyebrows. It is associated with intuition, imagination, and wisdom. When this chakra is balanced, we feel intuitively connected to our higher selves. The hue indigo is related to this chakra.

The Crown Chakra

Situated at the apex of the head, the crown, or seventh chakra is associated with spirituality and higher consciousness. When this chakra is balanced, we are aware of our connection with the Divine, as well as our own divinity. The hues purple and white are linked to this chakra.

The chakra system provides a map for our journey to wholeness. By understanding the role each chakra plays in our daily lives, we can start to heal the areas that are causing us pain and suffering. Once our chakras are balanced, we can live more fully in our purpose and power. And that includes our Holy Hot Visibility.

Understanding and working with the chakras has been an integral part of my personal journey, both personally and professionally. While living at an intentional spiritual community, for almost a decade, that was passed down from a direct lineage of Kriya Yoga masters, I was initiated in the lineage and practice of the Rainbow Path. This involved advanced technique where I would move the life force energy up and down my spine in circulations through each chakra. I learned to embody the very *tree of life* itself and, on a daily basis for these years (and well beyond, and continue to), experienced the dual sacred vortex of the Divine feminine and the Divine masculine energies combined as one.

I was raised as a "mutt" European with some labeling me a WASP (White Anglo-Saxon Protestant), though I resisted that term. I knew in my soul that I had lived many lifetimes and integrated diverse spiritual paths over time.

Christianity was my childhood faith, but seeking balance, I rebelled against its patriarchy and embraced Neopagan goddess worship after high school. My spiritual journey continued as I learned to listen through Zen Buddhism, then later embodied the light in Kriya Yoga. In my early 40s, I converted to tradition-rich Judaism, finding resonance in mystical Kabbalah's oneness with God.

Throughout it all, my timeless soul integrated each experience into a richer understanding of the Divine, leading me to resist labels and fully embrace the many lifetimes within.

The overarching theme in all my experiences has been a need to take the path of the mystic; to seek out the truth and Divine within myself that I was not separate from, to see into the etheric and be able to shapeshift my own energy (not as woo-woo as one might think), and understand the idea of heaven right here on Earth as much as possible. It is the desire to be congruent to unlimited consciousness in my daily life. To find divinity in the mundane. It doesn't switch off and it's not about taking days off. You become the mystic when you understand that your whole life is your service to the Divine oneness and start living that way.

When I first stepped out of the corporate world and onto the path of an entrepreneur, I was hiding behind a business brand. I longed to share my new meditation breath mantra or enlightenment experience I had on the airplane amid a bunch of sleeping passengers, but I didn't feel I had a place for blogging about it as I was not showing up as a personal brand. When I eventually did start talking about my spiritual path and integrating it in my business, I realized my ideal client was a soulful entrepreneur as well. And, as I learned more and more to show up for and as myself as both a sensual, embodied woman and a mystic, I discovered a synergy between some of the challenges I experienced around visibility and those of my clients.

This revelation led me to understand that...

It wasn't my fault that I had breasts, flowing hair, and long legs that excited men.

It wasn't my fault that my five astrological placements in Scorpio added to my passionate lifeforce energy, and that, when in my natural confidence, I shine brightly. My Scorpio intensity is an inherent part of me, fueling my vibrant spirit when I fully embrace my self-assurance. I do not view my passionate nature as a fault, but rather as a unique expression of the dynamic energy within me.

It wasn't my fault that when I danced I would share this energy. In fact, I never danced publicly until I was in my early forties, when I claimed the stage in a belly dance troupe to overcome showing up in my holy hot embodiment and tossing the shame of any views to the side. I'll tell you more about that in the next chapter.

Finally, it wasn't my fault that even a certain archetype of woman was mad at me when I shined with confidence at conferences and online.

The woman I knew I needed to work with was on her own journey of healing through increased visibility. She needed to emerge from isolation and disconnect, to find grounding after years or lifetimes trying to ascend the body through spiritual practices.

The work we must do is right here - embracing womanhood in our natural bodies, rewriting the false and toxic shame our matriarch Eve carried all these years as the original lover, mother, and woman.

My intention is to make life my act of devotion and share my inner holy experience in service to others. I have fully embraced the amalgamation of past oppression, shame imposed by the

Church and Patriarchy, and the cultural shadow that confronts us as women. This convergence has created a powerful and transformative storm within me. By expressing this deeply felt experience, I hope to transform it into liberation and light. My devotion is to take the weight of the past and alchemize it into freedom through full expression.

In this next part, I cover the patterns of invisibility and how to transform them into a sustainably spiritual and wholesomely holistic approach to the inner discovery, leading to more outer confidence and the ability to show up in life and business as ourselves.

Here, I will share the Holy Hot Principles I have learned and integrated to this point on my journey, translated into practical steps that you can apply to your own life and your personal branding in ways that feel safe, empowered, and authentic.

My Magic Maple and the Art of Presence

One night, after nursing my toddler to sleep, I had this realization that I cherish and adore to hanging out in what I affectionately call the "invisibility cave" – the space where no one in the world was viewing me and I was at one with my own presence, the presence that was beyond me and all the rooted allies and angels that surrounded me. This is the part of me that loves to meditate and dissolve back into my own little bubble of self, the space of recharge and the moment of being away from all the roles and hats I wear. It's being-with-my-soul-time, expanding in liberation with what's not in the world.

Where is your invisibility cave? It can be the meditation chair in your room, that special grove in the forest, or anywhere else you can energetically brought back to you in between client calls.

I have spent countless hours in meditation over the years. Lately, however, I haven't been very good about my practice. At all.

For a highly creative woman like myself, I understand the importance of going invisible at times to recharge. It allows me to tap into creativity, gain clarity, and find coherence within myself.

I even made a beautiful meditation corner in my bedroom for my practice. It has an authentic woven Flokati rug beneath a teal blue velvet wing chair that fits my legs in crisscross-applesauce – a favorite perch for upright meditations. Above me is my one-of-a-kind sphere of white feathers that is all girly and received from my former fortune teller client. Nearby is my antique secretary desk with a large silver Hamsa atop to bring beauty, cultural expression, and the remembrance of Divine protection beaming around.

I know I should be going there daily to refresh and recreate and, still, I don't. These days, I find myself barely awake with messy hair after a night of my co-sleeping cuddly toddler that always has a hand or foot extended to find some patch of me to connect with.

Sometimes my meditations are quick gratitude prayers with the morning sun zealously greeting me before I'm ready to pop the lids open, and yet I endeavor to count my blessings through groggy toddler speak and ruffled bedding. If I can get my instant coffee with coconut superfood creamer for an on-the-go format so I can feel like I might have a chance to conquer the tasks of the day.

That space is my cherished happy place, reminiscent of the times I used to retreat to the pockets of the meadow beneath the craggy mountain on my grandparents' land when I was very young.

It is a feeling of safety, and rootedness. That is what a happy place feels like, and that is what I desire you to find within yourself, that you can travel with anywhere you like. This includes the journey of being visible, when we can reconnect with our secret inner dwelling place in the face of judgment and unkindness that lingers in the world.

While I could easily start the steps at the crown chakra, since you are (most likely) a conscious soul who has already done a lot of work and are here to learn more about embodiment, I have decided to begin with the traditional and primordial starting place: the root of our existence.

———————

.

So now I want to take you back to the roots, literally, to a space we dwell as home and the places our bodies will rest forever. From this place, I'd love to tell you a story about a friend of mine who was deeply rooted and some of what she taught me about my happy place within and feeling rooted in safety in the world.

When I was quite young, perhaps around seven years old, and lived in the rain forests of the Pacific Northwest, there was a beloved big leaf maple I named my "Magic Maple Tree."

Because, of course, she was magic.

And she taught me to understand my own. She brought me peace, understanding, and reflection of myself. She would give back to me strength and a place of refuge which I learned to be the wholeness of presence.

I felt a safety and groundedness and connection that led me to a sense of belonging. Deeply rooted – there before I came and likely after I left – my Magic Maple Tree was dancing with flexible permanence. She was also full of understanding, and the quiet energy we shared allowed me to feel seen even while I felt invisible in the rest of the world, where I could be heard as a reliable and unconditional presence in the foundation of my well-being.

I merged with the tree.

I was one with the tree.

In fact, my tree taught me a lot about the steps in Part 2 of this book, which I wrote from my understanding from this inward connected place. It is the place where we can deeply discover ourselves.

Since my tree was quiet and would always listen, she is where I would go when I didn't feel understood by my family. It was where I learned I wouldn't necessarily feel understood in the world as a highly sensitive and empathic type and would need to learn to let go of others' energies and acquire the skills to give them back to the earth and root myself in my own being.

I used to sit in the mulch and dry decomposed leaves to rest my back against its thick and sturdy trunk and speak and dialog and vent and commune in the unspoken language of the heart. I would feel my place in the world from this one small vantage point. I told all my problems and all my secrets to her. She always listened and always forgave, and she never judged.

I remember staring up at her branches and imagining myself climbing her; then, at her invitation, I would go up, up, the different avenues of her branches, leading me to different views and vantage points of her epic lookout and imagining that this was how the guides and guardian angels look down and see us. It was the freedom to use my body and strength to go somewhere that no one else would be in that moment, to go somewhere that no one else may ever go. I was empowered in my own little bubble of creation.

Her leaves waved in feathery grace and brought me a sense of visual beauty and solace. For fun, I would whirl the two-seeded pod helicopters and watch them vertically dance to meet their final destination on the ground. She was an insatiable beauty and pure entertainment.

The tree nurtured me, and gave me reminders of sustenance and stability. It reached down into the earth and was held and reached up to the heavens. The tree reminded me of my life purpose... I was to be a bridge for these two, just like the tree.

I loved my tree.

Trees stand for steadiness; they just ARE. The big trees go deeply rooted into our creation, yet, as we do in our soul's evolution, they reach for the sky, the heavens, the Divine. Grounded, steady, full of equanimity, presence, no matter what phase of growth they are in, they are always reaching for the light. May we be more like the trees.

The tree was my best and most understanding friend or spirit family member, but sometimes good stories have sad endings.

When I was eight, my parents, desiring to be less isolated from friends and suburban life, made the decision to move to town. It was like having to go into the world and start again, without her branches and leaves and solace of shade to hide in and under. I was heartbroken that I would never be with my Magic Maple Tree again.

And yet... I realized I was taking her teachings with me.

Over the years, even as an adult living in California, whenever I visited family in Oregon I would drive down the country lane to Magic Maple Tree and see how much she had grown and view her from the road in front of the house. Even though I had to leave, I had received so much about embodying grace and beauty, and being deeply rooted and restful in my own quiet presence.

This was the introspective, introverted part of me that recharged in my own resplendence by embodying the tree. I learned presence, self-witnessing, self-talk and the beginnings of learning to pray. I could say my spiritual path began at my tree.

When it comes to being seen in the world, it's so easy to imagine what another person is thinking. Since people are quick to judge, create projections of their own experiences, or have vision tinted by their own egoic positioning, they are what we think of when we are visible. We are not labeled by the tree or the animal or the river. It is only the "other" and the inner voice of ourselves.

This is where we must master our own self-talk when the haters come to hate. When we put something out into the world and family or a family member doesn't "approve," when your friends think you're crazy, or when the negative comments on social media start flooding in.

We can identify all the many places where there are opportunities for our insecurities to arise. This is when we must tap into our sovereignty and speak with our inner Magic Maple Tree – that space that is here to witness whatever we need to witness.

This aspect in us can be strengthened whenever we go within to remember the uniqueness of who we are becoming. Meditation over the years has taught me this and I utilize the flow of business and following the guidance of new projects as if I were sitting at the base of a tree... listening... letting the wind twirl my tresses.

I discovered it was beyond my Magic Maple Tree. It was about my relationship with our Creator. The one and only lasting and real relationship we have.

The tree taught me to have a relationship with the Divine that was bigger than me, bigger than the "other," and seemingly outside of me, yet also within me, flowing through me as the light floods my cells and becomes me.

The tree was my first spiritual teacher, and the beginning of my path to meditation and attuning to the presence of the Divine. Even today, my tree brings me back to that magical space of safety anytime I need to call on that rooted presence within me and feel the ground beneath me.

And that's what we are talking about:

HOLY. *YOU ARE THAT.*

In all of your shame, your humanity, your soul.

Back to the merging place, where we are rooted and the space of how we are eternal.

I can only go this high by being also right here, right now. In my learning, being deeply grounded helps the tree withstand the wildest winds and waylay being uprooted. Having deep roots while reaching for the sky helps us to aspire but stay connected to the earth and our sense of embodiment no matter how high we might go, because we are nourished by the place within.

We are both embodied and Divine. And may this whispering remind and awaken the wind may rustle the leaves of your tree, as you are both deeply rooted.

As you are and become heaven and Earth in human form.

Both holy... and hot.

Cultivating Safety in Being Seen & Stepping Out in Wholeness

Think about the times when you want to put something out there... your art, your "baby"... that thing you have journeyed with and prepared to share with the world.

It certainly brings up vulnerability and we almost feel naked, like it's unsafe to expose our aspects of soul depth. Let's look at that vulnerability.

This is about YOU coming forward more – that part of your soul or psyche that has been hidden or tucked away, happily living in the invisibility cave or closet. Maybe it's been tucked away since those tender, innocent years of childhood, when perhaps what you shared was not understood, cherished, or validated.

Maybe it was even ridiculed, or you felt shame around sharing this piece, so you learned to stuff these parts of you within yourself. You kept them away to keep you safe.

If you're on the path as a creative or spiritual entrepreneur, you've had to let it out at some point and get out in the world as a necessity. Once you've done that, once you've allowed it to shine in the light, well, there will be the next thing that will require you to become even more visible.

Maybe it's publishing that book, but then you have to share it on social media and be available for interviews on podcasts; maybe it's even speaking on that stage. Then, it's the next book that maybe goes even deeper.

Sharing my art used to be extremely difficult because I felt like I was baring my soul. It wasn't until the past few years that I even imagined selling it, as if I'd be parting with my little creative babies. I had to make the shift and know that I can always make more as I am blessed with prolific creative currency. Of course if there is an original piece of art that is just too close to my heart, I can always sell the prints. But as I create more and mature in my own being, I have come to be at peace with creating and giving away my gifts.

I recall that moment, many years ago, when I first posted a photo of myself on Facebook, how I held my breath, scared of showing this aspect of myself. Even worse was when I started making videos for social media... What if I didn't have anything to say? What if no one had anything to say about my share? *And... people were looking at me!*

When we show up and allow ourselves to be seen, we interact with more people and more stimuli, info, and energy comes our way. This includes sharing ourselves more deeply. Of course we are going to be judged (even though we don't know the half of who is judging us or what they are thinking). And let's remember the things people are judging for are usually reflecting the way about themselves.

You can transmute the idea of judgment by allowing others' wounds to fall by the wayside so you can step forward be seen and share your gifts. By transmuting the notion of judgment, we can let go of others' woundedness and negative projections, allowing them to fade away. This liberation enables us to step forward, fully seen, and wholeheartedly share our unique gifts with the world. This is a growth edge – a process. It doesn't have to be your business what they think of you. When you can bring this awareness to the ego, the little self, give it some love, and allow your soul to come forth in its true alignment, it becomes much easier to dance out of your comfort zone and break through to your next level.

I remember a retreat in Costa Rica I attended when I was the photographer. When it was my turn to talk about being visible in our businesses as the radiant women we are, I looked around the intimate circle of ten, sitting cross-legged and barefoot in the breezy, open-air yoga studio, and had this moment of, *Wow, I'm going to take up their time, I better have something worthwhile to share.* I also noticed how odd it felt to have so much attention on me. It was thrilling in one sense, but in another it was unsettling, and I wanted to run out of the room.

After I spoke, I got positive feedback, with one of the ladies, her eyes filling with tears, how meaningful what I shared was for her. In that moment, I realized sharing from my heart what was meaningful to me could help others – even if it was just one small thing, for just one person. In this case, ironically, I was talking about why it's important to allow yourself to be visible in the world as we move past our fears. In this moment, I knew I was enough.

Wouldn't it be worth it if your purposeful work could positively change the trajectory for just one person? Sometimes breaking it down into bite-sized pieces can relieve the pressure of making a massive impact on a large audience.

We have to find the path forward from this inner place to the doorway out of the cave so we can finally be revealed to the light of the world. In this revealing process, we are seen, we are witnessed, and we now have a mirror of our being to understand itself in a different way through the lens of sharing it and self-expressing.

And yes, a lot can come up when this happens – perhaps our fears, or concern of being criticized, or even being completely ignored. What if we feel betrayed? Abandoned? What if what we share isn't enough?

This is the work: to understand how we can heal the parts of ourselves that have remained in the shadowy parts of our vulnerability. Being visible is letting yourself shine through the places you have been keeping safe in the shadows.

This aspect of being visible is associated with our feelings of safety and security – physically, metaphorically, emotionally, and spiritually. It reminds us of our most basic and primal needs and even activates our survival instincts triggering the fight-or-flight responses.

When we have these things come up and notice tightness in our bodies it is important to have new awareness but to also be careful that we don't have shame for the feelings that arise. When we can identify with what comes up, that is when we can be the alchemist of our own reality and lift it to a higher cause. This can be transmuting through prayer or taking action in overcoming the stuff that holds us back.

Let's go deeper into that.

You Hold the Riverbed for the River

When we feel scared, we might sense a lack of support. To blossom and become who we are meant to be, we need our roots firmly planted in the earth, reaching up to the sun, and spreading our petals. The healing of the feminine starts with the relationship to the Mother, not necessarily our biological mother, but the "Great Mother" of creation. With a sense of grounding and gravity, she fully holds us, allowing us to transmute and process our energy and fears, empowering us to embrace our truth.

The mother represents our genesis, the origin of the root from which we emerge.

When we are connected to our root, we feel safe and connected, not to only ourselves but the environment around us. This is the sacred space where our desires can manifest, as we must anchor ourselves physically on Earth and connect with our rootedness, particularly if we are journeying towards higher consciousness on the spiritual path. It is a process of self-regulation, where we navigate through fears and find solace in an anchor that helps us weather the stormy energies. Through this process, our anxieties and fears can be transmuted into transformative forces.

Over time, we can evolve through the layers out of that Invisibility Cave.

We have the power to transform the chains that hold us back and restrict our ability to fully express ourselves and shine as we are meant to. One of my favorite tools for this is grounding deeply within ourselves, connecting both with Earth and the etheric realm. It begins with intimate self-observation and self-witnessing, providing the support we need to navigate whatever challenges arise. Cultivating this self-connection requires time, practice, and patience.

One way to begin with this is to have more awareness and ask yourself, How do you feel in your body when you share who you are and what you do?

In order to claim your sovereign space, create a deep sense of presence in your body and beingness. Feeling rooted and safe allows your lifeforce energy of creation to blossom.

Your root chakra is the foundation for the other chakras to do their thing and be fully activated at their fullest potential. This is especially important in having a thriving and prosperous business as you are expanding your earthly potential.

When you are activated and clear in your root chakra, you create a foundation upon which your other chakras can use their full potential to create the life you desire to see around you.

This is especially important when you want to grow a thriving, abundant business. If you are sacrificing the relationship and needs of your body, you are limiting your earthly potential.

When you allow your root energy to move through your spine's channel to your crown chakra, you become expanded and powerful in your ability to create.

Your Path Through the First Gateway

Just as the root anchors a tree and provides nourishment, the first chakra serves as the foundation upon which your online presence can flourish as you all for the sustenance of the sun to fill you with lifeforce.

In the fast-paced digital world, it's easy to feel overwhelmed, exposed, and uncertain about putting yourself out there. This space invites you to heal any wounds of insecurity, fear, or instability that may be holding you back. By nurturing and strengthening your root, you create a solid ground from which you can confidently navigate the online realm.

To establish safety, it's crucial to ground yourself in authenticity and self-assurance. We'll deepen in this as we climb the ladder of the 7 Gateways.

As you embrace your unique gifts, experiences, and voice as you craft your online presence, you will cultivate a sense of trust in your abilities and the value you bring to the table.

By honoring your truth and staying rooted in your authentic self, you attract genuine connections and resonate with your ideal audience.

Security in the online world comes from developing a strong and consistent personal brand. There is important foundational work to do such as clarifying your core message, values, and mission, aligning them with your online presence.

This helps you stand out amidst the buzz and establish yourself as an expert in your niche. Focus on delivering high-quality creative content that educates, inspires, and serves your audience. By consistently delivering value, you also build that legendary trust and loyalty – the "know-like-and-trust" mojo, creating a secure foundation for your online visibility.

Stability is essential for long-term success and sustainability in the online realm. Rootedness is also the sphere of crafting clear goals, creating a content strategy quarter to quarter, and establishing routines that support your visibility efforts.

By healing and nurturing your root, The First Gateway, you create a solid and secure foundation for your online visibility. As you establish safety, security, and stability, you will feel more grounded and confident in sharing your authentic self with the world.

Your online presence is an extension of your unique essence, and by embracing the energy of your rootedness, you lay the groundwork for a vibrant and flourishing presence, just like Magic Maple Tree taught me so well.

Rooted Practice

· When you wake in the morning, take a pause to be present in your body. I like to feel a gentle smile of gratitude as I gently feel into her.

· Send roots down from your spine into the earth. Ground yourself in the physical world so you may create a bridge for all you desire to manifest here.

- Take a drop of sandalwood or patchouli essential oil into your hands and rub them together. Take a deep inhale of the aroma and be present with the way your body responds. Give gratitude for your physical senses that allow you to experience the fullness of life.

- Take a moment to connect with your physical needs and ask, "What do I need to support my body today?" Journal what you notice...

When you go deeper with your body and allow the uncomfortable to be what it is, you stop sacrificing and harming yourself by striving and pushing with the mind.

Your soul wants to be seen, known, and felt. It's a natural instinct for our souls to share themselves and circulate in the world.

It's a breath of fresh air when we allow ourselves to bloom. Allowing ourselves to bloom is like a refreshing breath of air. It requires a conscious, attentive, and present mindset, akin to nurturing a rose and watching it grow. Similarly, we must allow our petals to gracefully unfold, embracing our visibility and basking in the radiance of the sun. In doing so, we share our unique fragrance, allowing ourselves to be fully known and appreciated.

Your Holy Hot Visibility Action

Building a rock-solid brand foundation is like constructing a magnificent fortress that towers above the digital landscape. It all begins by unearthing the treasures within – your core values that illuminate the path to your Brand Archetypes. These gems hold the keys for you to dig deep into the depths of your being, unearthing the treasures that define your essence and fuel your passion and unlock your brand's true potential.

Branding is truly an inside job that starts right here, right now, coming from the stability you are creating on the bedrock of *you*, as the foundation of your brand. This is about who we are, how we fit into the world, and how we embrace ourselves and what is already true for us to become magnetic in the vibration of our true essence.

Your core values are already in you and already you as the heart and soul of your brand. They serve as the guiding ideals that characterize you and your values. Think of them as the North Star that leads your brand on its journey that directs your brand's journey, ensuring that every decision, every message, and every interaction is aligned with your true purpose. Take the time to reflect on what truly matters to you, what ignites your spirit, and what legacy you wish to leave behind. Let these reflections guide you in selecting your top two to three core values that will serve as the grounding of your brand.

Brand archetypes are like the colorful characters that bring your brand to life. They represent the distinct personality and style of your brand, adding depth and intrigue. They are the secret sauce that captures the hearts and minds of your audience with storytelling, both visually and in terms of messaging, that is understood by the psyche.

While core values are the soil of your brand's identity, brand archetypes are the magical ingredients that make your brand unforgettable. Together, they create a harmonious symphony that connects with your audience and distinguishes your brand from the crowd.

Imagine your brand as a vibrant tapestry, woven with the threads of your core values and adorned with the vibrant colors of your brand archetypes. This tapestry becomes a powerful beacon, attracting like-minded souls who are inspired by your purpose and vision.

Learning your top core values and your brand archetypes is an introspective process that requires self-reflection and deep exploration (and a few steps and tools help the pathway).

Here is a step-by-step guide to help you uncover your core values:

1. Self-Reflection

Always begin from this space because you are the origin of your innerverse. Set aside dedicated time for self-reflection. Find a quiet and comfortable space where you can be alone with your thoughts. Reflect on your life experiences, beliefs, and what truly matters to you. Consider the moments that have brought you the most joy, fulfillment, and a sense of purpose. Jot down any values or qualities that resonate with you during this reflection.

2. Identify Key Themes and Prioritize Your Values

Look for patterns or recurring themes among the values you identified in the previous step. Group similar values together and notice any common threads that emerge. This will help you identify overarching themes that represent your core values. Review the themes and values you have identified and prioritize them based on their importance to you. Ask yourself which values are non-negotiable and deeply ingrained in your being. Choose the top values that resonate the most with you and reflect who you are at your core.

3. Take a Brand Archetype Assessment

There are various online quizzes and assessments available that can help you identify your brand archetypes including the one on my website at to unveil your #1 Brand Archetype: **www.ProsperityBranding.com/quiz.** This assessment is a series of questions designed to uncover your brand's personality traits and characteristics. Answer the questions honestly and intuitively to get the most accurate results. Once you have completed the archetype assessment, review and analyze the results. Look for patterns and common themes among the archetypes that resonate with you. Pay attention to the archetypes that align closely with your brand's values, purpose, and desired image.

4. Vision Your Values

Imagine living a life guided by each of your selected values. Visualize how it aligns with your aspirations, goals, and the impact you want to make in the world. Consider the level of fulfillment and authenticity each value brings to your life. This process will help you validate and confirm your top core values. Review your selected core values and make any necessary refinements. Ensure that they are authentic to who you are and in alignment with your vision and purpose. Be open to revisiting and refining your values as you continue to grow and evolve.

5. Embody Your Values

Once you have identified your top core values, it's essential to integrate them into your daily life and decision-making. Let your values guide your actions, choices, and interactions with others. Embodying your values will bring a sense of authenticity, purpose, and fulfillment to your personal and professional endeavors.

Remember, discovering your core values is a deeply personal journey. Take your time, believe in your gut, and give yourself permission to explore and evolve. Your core values will guide you toward a life and brand that are true to you.

As you weave your core values into the fabric of your brand, remember that authenticity is the key. Allow your true self to shine through in every aspect of your brand's existence.

Infuse your visuals with your unique aesthetic, infuse your messaging with your genuine voice, and infuse your experiences with your heartfelt connection. Embrace the power of vulnerability and transparency, for it is in these qualities that your audience will find solace and resonance.

In this grand adventure, you will inspire others with your brand's story. Paint vivid pictures that transport them to a world where their dreams align with your aspirations. Be audacious in your vision, daring to dream bigger and bolder. And amidst the pursuit of your dreams, always remember to honor yourself, practicing self-care and dancing to the rhythm of your soul's needs. By nourishing your own well-being, you become a beacon of light, radiating a magnetic energy that draws others toward your brand's mission.

So, my lovely visionary, let your brand's foundation be a testament to your true essence. Embrace the challenges, celebrate the victories, and let your unique voice and values guide you on this extraordinary journey.

I raise my kombucha to your creating a world where authenticity reigns, and where brands are built upon a foundation of purpose, passion, and unwavering integrity as yourself.

Remember to keep the flame of inspiration burning bright, for it is through this flame that your authentic brand story will unfold.

1st Gateway Journal Prompts

1. Take a moment to look back at your history and upbringing. How have the experiences and background shaped who you are today including your values? How can you align these aspects with the core of your brand to create a foundation?

2. Consider the values that define your individuality. How can you translate these values into the essence of your brand infusing them into your brand messaging and offerings?

3. Reflect on any wounds or traumas that might be impacting the foundation and visibility of your brand. How can you bring healing to these wounds to create a more genuine brand identity?

4. Delve into the idea of stability as it relates to establishing a foundation, for your brands growth and success. How can you build a base that allows your brand to thrive? In what ways does this stability contribute to increased visibility and overall success?

5. Take some time to contemplate your relationship with money and abundance. How does this relationship influence the foundation and visibility of your brand? What steps can you take to develop a mindset, around abundance that supports the growth of your brand?

GATEWAY 2:

PASSION & CREATIVITY

From Uncreative to Creative

Abundance, Sensuality, Vitality

"Soul work is not a high road. It's a deep fall into an unforgiving darkness that won't let you go until you find the song that sings you home."
— McCall Erickson

A couple of years ago, at forty-two, I was naturally giving birth to my third son. Blessed with a natural (and a little surprising) conception, especially at my age and much that I had been through as a mother; in fact, it seemed a little "immaculate." I had started out thinking of going the hospital route, due to societal whisperings that I was geriatric and "safer" to birth there. However, I longed to have another natural birth in the hot tub nestled in palms and tropical plants in the backyard of our Santa Barbara home. I longed to do it in the primordial ways of the natural feminine mother and even had fantasies of unassisted birth like I imagined having in other lifetimes.

Making my three precious sons has been the most potent, mind-blowing adventure - the ultimate Divine gift of co-creation. Pregnancy and birth have humbled me, making me feel simultaneously powerful yet also a student in Earth School. Through the endless lessons learned in channeling this lifeforce, I grasped that I am but a small "c" creator. Creativity flows through me, guided by the Miraculous One's unseen hand merging science and infinite possibility. Though my role felt big, creation happened not because of me, but through me. My body and this process have taught me what it means to be human, vulnerable, and in awe of the divine intelligence so far beyond my own. I am endlessly grateful for the privilege of co-creating three lives and gaining a deeper wisdom in the process.

And, if I feel stuck, it doesn't come through me as easily.

In moments of panic when the pain became overwhelming, my labor often stalled at six centimeters dilated. The fear that the intensity would tear my body apart caused me to tense up and resist the natural process. But when I got out of my own head, trusted my body, and remembered to breathe, things started moving again.

It's like reaching orgasm - by letting go, breathing deeply, and allowing the creative energy to flow through you, the contractions can build in a natural rhythm. Just as composing a symphony requires getting into a creative "flow zone," birthing relies on dropping into the body's wisdom and letting go of fear. My body knew what to do, I just needed to get out of my own way.

My husband started reading Psalms out loud while I writhed in the water tub, moving through the intense primordial birthing pains. The heavens parted, I nearly had a part in splitting the seas as my son was birthed into the warm waters of the blow-up pool in our bedroom, and shortly after I touched the top of the tiny miracle of his head.

Our first mother, Eve, and all the women throughout time and space as the lover-mother passed through as my baby squirmed in my arms and began to vocalize his voice for the first time as the angels played their ethereal trumpets of welcoming.

While I realize not every woman's birth story is like mine, nor did every woman who longed to be a mother get to be one, I share my story as my creation in this world, beyond any medium of art or any perfected line of prose.

As an embodied mother three times over, I am aware of my feminine lifeforce being capable of sharing what my soul desires. Becoming comfortable with your "hot" or sensual, sexual energy and creative lifeforce is the cornerstone upon which all of life and ideas are brought into being!

Natural Magnetism Vs. Performance Exhaustion

Yes, we will "go there" about the role of innate allure and magnetism in visibility. There is a vast difference between being rooted in genuine self-expression and embracing your true essence and relying on performance and trying to forcefully attract attention through artificial means.

Authentic, natural allure and magnetism is pure and stems from a deep sense of self-acceptance and self-love. It is about embracing and expressing your unique qualities, passions, and values without trying to conform to societal expectations or perform for others. When you show up authentically, it naturally radiates a magnetic energy that attracts others who resonate with your essence. It's the essence of the Second Gateway!

Authentic magnetism is an emanation of inner creativity, confidence, and alignment. It is not about seeking validation or approval from others but rather owning and celebrating who you are. When you are confident in your own skin and believe in your worth and value, it exudes an irresistible energy that draws people towards you. This confidence comes from within and is not dependent on external validation or performance.

Authentic visibility focuses on building genuine connections with others. It is about being present and fully engaged in your interactions, rather than trying to impress or manipulate others. When you approach visibility with a genuine desire to connect, listen, and understand, it creates a space for authentic relationships to blossom. This kind of connection is far more powerful and sustainable than surface-level interactions based on performance.

When you show up as your true self and consistently deliver value, it establishes trust with your audience or community and people are naturally drawn to individuals who are genuine, transparent, and trustworthy. By focusing on authenticity rather than performing, you cultivate long-term relationships and a loyal following.

Authentic visibility is fueled by a sustainable energy that comes from aligning with your true essence. It allows you to tap into your natural talents, passions, and strengths, which can create a lasting impact without going into burnout, as often happens when you come from a pushing energy, trying to be that which you are not. Instead, it becomes an inherent part of your being, making your visibility effortless and sustainable in the long run.

Relying on performance and pushing for brand attention may yield short-term results but lacks the soulful depth and genuine impact that your authentic visibility brings. It can create a sense of inauthenticity and disconnect, both within yourself and with your audience, akin to a shallow stream that dries up under the scorching sun, leaving behind only a temporary illusion of abundance.

By embracing your authentic natural lifeforce and magnetism in visibility, you cultivate a genuine presence, build meaningful connections, and create a lasting impact. It is about shining brightly as your true self, rather than trying to conform to external expectations or resorting to artificial tactics. When you embody your authentic essence, you naturally attract the right people and opportunities, allowing your visibility to flourish in a way that is aligned and downright more pleasurable as your truest self.

As you arrive in the glorious vitality of this aspect of your being, you are invited to activate the full potential of your creative life force energy so you can feel safe to share your message with the world and be visible, heard, and expressed. When you claim embodiment and pleasure as a strategy and allow for its power to move in supportive ways, your life will change in courageous, powerful ways as you unleash your unstoppable birthright as a powerhouse of sacred luminous creativity.

My journey has been occasionally a painful one around the innocence of the sexual lifeforce that exudes from my being. I am simply a human and have always been rich in innate procreative erotic femininity; however, I have learned to hide it, conceal it, tame it, numb it, and all the other things to not attract too much attention. Can you relate?

One of the big fears of women, especially those on the spiritual journey, is getting unwanted attention from unwanted and unsolicited voyeurs, viewers, stalkers, and trolls. And I cannot even imagine how intensified this is for women surviving the horrors of being violated as a child or an adult in any way. That level of tenderness and healing is a very unique journey, and my prayer is that eventually every woman has the freedom to feel alive in her sensual pleasure and God-given nature of eros, the vitality of life itself.

Whether it be a result of past lives or nuances of unwanted attention from boys or men in this one, I have experienced the huge polarity of wanting to be seen and also wanting to disappear into oneness with creation. I have personally faced the challenge of feeling truly liberated and comfortable with being seen, as I yearned to dissolve certain aspects of my physicality and merge them with the essence of my soul, seeking a sense of oneness.

Unleashing My Inner Dance: Conquering Another Layer of Fear on the Path to Visibility

Dancing has been a beautiful bridge of embodying my prayer.

I fell in love with belly dancing in my early twenties. Every Wednesday night, The Old World Deli would feature a lineup of dancers that made you feel like you were in some alternative exotic universe. The dimmed audience, cast in colored stage lights, would engage in hissing and *zaghareeting* (the trilling of the tongue expressing excitement and joy of the moment) as the enchantment of the dancers fell upon all.

I wanted to take up the art form and it immediately brought back ancient remembrances... Call it past life if you want, my soul identified deeply with this feminine serpenty sacred dance and my inner girl who loves to endlessly spin, twirl, and make worlds out of nothing came completely alive in it.

But I never wanted to dance on stage at the Old World Deli. I wanted to grapevine with my sisters in a circle of goddesses from another realm and take turns honoring one woman at a time with a solo unrehearsed *taqsim*. What felt real for me was to share the dance in a sacred space of women, since it was foundationally a dance for other women. Yet at the same time, I wanted my privacy as a dancer. It was something I didn't want to share.

And then my soul knew I was to share my sacred private dance one time and do it in public as some kind of full-circle karmic completion. I know that sounds woo-woo, but it's what I was given.

This time, I knew belly dancing, even with a troupe, in public would help me overcome another layer of the onion of being seen.

I did finally dance publicly to overcome some of my karma in being seen in my sensuality. Though very tastefully done in a group at a restaurant and music club in downtown Santa Barbara, I gave it my all and allowed myself to feel and BE fully beautiful in my embodied, creative, feminine lifeforce energy. In other words, after years of hiding, I finally found the courage to put myself out there – and it shimmied with a hip scarf and some catchy music.

The class with my troupe was gorgeous – I loved learning all the different moves and hearing the music. We moved in unison like the synchronization of the circle dances from long ago in Oregon, and even farther back from some distant time. The best part was how good it made me feel about myself.

I felt confident and sexy. I felt like I could be seen in my colorful expression in this way.

I remember my heart racing and my palms sweating as I undulated up to the stage with my dancing sisters.

But I went out there and did it anyway.

And you know what?

I didn't die. In fact, it was amazing. The feeling of joy and freedom that came with dancing in front of an audience was unbeatable (pun intended).

Turns out, belly dancing was exactly what I needed to help me boost my confidence and get over more of my fear of being seen.

I started to relax and really enjoy myself. I became more comfortable with being in my own skin. And eventually, I began to feel like a confident, vibrant woman instead of a scared little girl.

Belly dancing also helped me become more comfortable with my body. Despite being various shapes and sizes over the years as a mama of three, I never really felt like my weight was an issue unless I started comparing myself to the other women in my class. But, slowly but surely, I realized that there's no one "right" way to look – we all come in different shapes and sizes, and that's what makes us beautiful. Belly dancing helped me appreciate my curves and learn to love my body just the way it is.

It's about having the tenacity to continue to experience new things outside my comfort zone. And, each time, I come away feeling a little bit more confident and a little bit more alive.

When I look back at how far I've come, it's amazing to see how much one experience can impact your life in such a delightful way. If you're struggling with confidence or anxiety, don't be afraid to try something new – you never know where it might lead you.

Allow yourself to experiment with different forms of self-expression, such as writing, art, or dance, to discover authentic modes of that creative lifeforce to flourish. Allow yourself to express your thoughts, emotions, and desires without fear of judgment and enjoy the embrace of human vulnerability as you share your true self with others, attracting those who resonate with your depth of natural magnetic authenticity.

Transcendent versus Embodied Spirituality

Belly dancing aside, the spiritual path I've walked in the past has been one of much oneness and silence where my spiritual ego wanted to ascend to leave this body to unite with the oneness of the Divine.

That part knows I am a spiritual being while existing in this flesh form – and that we came into life alone and exit it the same way – and, well, it can feel lonely. And, even in this, the mystic desires continuous search of oneness with the Divine.

In truth, we are human animals who want to run wild naked in the woods under the starlit sky with our skin painted with mud.

At least I have at times. It's important to remember our wild, imperfect selves as we are meant to be in a tribe as part of the oneness of humanity.

There is also the part of us, as spiritual beings, that doesn't want to be seen as a personal brand. We don't want too much attention, vanity, or me-me-me... which is exactly why it is so important for us to integrate the two and be who we are at our core – both hot and holy– human and soul!

I used to have so much shame around being human and couldn't do enough to cast off the awful and false projection of "original sin," which wasn't even in the original story of Eve and Adam in the Garden but something added later by the oppressive church to keep people in fear, guilt, and shame so they would go to the "powers that be" to wash ourselves.

When we acknowledge the times we've missed the mark and learn to forgive and heal ourselves, we cleanse our souls gently in the rivers of atonement (at-one-ment) and keep moving forward. No one is condemned for having a sex drive and experiencing desires. While this book won't delve into the specifics of how we harness or channel lust and creative life force, one thing is certain: when we consciously apply the power of creativity to our lives, relationships, businesses, and spiritual path, a new level of vibrant and creative living unfolds repeatedly.

Spirituality wanted to become the pillar and center of my life. I started to heal my shame, take a real look at how my ego liked to run the show and the places my shadow needed to come into the light, and allow myself to have a voice again and be seen by others.

A lot of my earlier path was to disappear into meditation and deep-dive into practices of transcending the body. It wasn't said outwardly, but I came to learn through the dogma and ideology of various paths and spiritual cultures that the hierarchy of what was more popular or heavenly began and ended with the upper chakras. I was misled for a while on the path that they were clearly more Godly and holy than the lower ones...

Raised eyebrows and mmm-hmmms...

I came to be a little brainwashed in certain spiritual spheres that the red-orangey chakras – that sexual one – was considered one to need to be harnessed in proper ways and not even talked about so much; the hush-hushed, unwanted one gets pushed aside from the more pious bunch, like the blues, violets, and rosy pink ones.

I spent a few years as part of a spiritual group that was devoted to bringing the energy up and out to try and evolve or transcend to a heavenly realm because that is more real and true since the body would eventually die.

Together, we chanted, "I am not the body" – and while understanding that we are more than the body is uber-important for many people on the path, I was learning to disconnect from my body to a degree that was not serving me.

Later, I realized I had always lived somewhat out-of-body, inhabiting ethereal realms. Since childhood, I walked around in a fantastical inner world, guided by vivid spirit guides, speaking mystical languages. My chakras extended from my heart upward, as I often felt I floated in otherworldly planes. I was more attuned to the mystical than the physical, dwelling in imaginal realms beyond the mundane. Grounding in earthly existence was a challenge, when my spirit felt so at home in the heavens. Over time, I learned to integrate the ethereal with the embodied, bridging my airy consciousness with tangible reality.

I tended to disembody due to trauma I believe occurred pre-birth and as a newborn infant. This led me to "check out" and disconnect from my physical form. Over time, I realized wholeness required embracing my body fully - being rooted in the physical while also exploring higher realms. My path became about integrating the spiritual and the earthly, learning self-love and acceptance in this vessel to heal past wounds. I had to bridge ethereal travels with being grounded in order to find balance and full presence. My journey led me to reclaim and inhabit my body with compassion after living so long out of embodiment.

Spiritual Sexual Shaming

Shame is an incredibly powerful emotion that can prevent us from fully shining in the world. It is the feeling that we are not good enough, that we are unworthy of love and respect.

Did you know that the etymology of the word "shame" comes from Old English meaning "to cover"? Need I say more about how shame leads to invisibility and covering our light?

Shame can cause us to doubt ourselves, to second-guess our choices, and to withdraw from the world and want to stay covered, which isn't convenient to getting your purposeful calling and that dream that lives inside of you out. Healing shame requires us to first recognize it for what it is.

Shame loves to hide, so it can be difficult to see. Once we are able to see shame for what it is, we can begin to work through it. This might mean reaching out for support from a therapist or a trusted friend.

One facet of shame is "unwanted exposure" which oftentimes visibility can subconsciously or unconsciously bring into our experience.

Unwanted exposure, linked to feelings of shame, often comes to mind when we don't feel perfect on video or in our way of being in our visibility efforts.

It refers to unintentionally drawing attention to ourselves in ways we wish to avoid, especially in public. This may be a given if you aren't feeling comfortable getting visible in the first place. An example is moments like tripping or spilling something exemplify this.

It could manifest during a live webinar, where you stumble over your words or experience technical difficulties, leaving you feeling embarrassed in front of your people.

Or you launch a new product, and despite your best efforts, it receives negative feedback or that hater or doesn't get the views or likes you hoped, triggering self-doubt and feelings of inadequacy.

Maybe you share a vulnerable and personal story in a blog post or social media, and while some people resonate with it, others criticize or misunderstand your message, making you question your authenticity in the first place.

It can cut like a knife even more so when it's something personal like your creative work and someone makes a snarky or critical comment that weighs heavily on your confidence and leaves you questioning your artistic abilities.

The key is to recognize that everyone experiences moments of vulnerability and imperfection, and practicing self-compassion and self-kindness is crucial to navigate these challenges and helping us detach from shame and self-criticism as we continue to grow and thrive in the creative entrepreneurial journey.

We are not gods! Hugging our vulnerability with grace liberates us from the shackles of shame, growing in empathy and connections with others. Reframing these incidents as opportunities for growth empowers us to face the world with authenticity. Embracing our flaws and vulnerabilities with self-acceptance allows us to build resilience and confidence. By doing so, we break free from shame and nurture self-growth.

It might mean doing some inner work to uncover the roots of our shame. And it might mean practicing that self-compassion and self-care in ways we had never traversed. Healing from shame is not an easy process, but it is worth it. When we heal our shame, we open the possibility of shining more brightly in the world, with less fear.

We become more confident, more authentic, and more radiant. We show up in the world as our true loving selves, and we make a difference in the lives of others.

Shame in the spiritual realm is a multifaceted dichotomy of egoic overlay in the name of being spiritual. It can be disguised and directed in the name of being "spiritual," even though we know that is coming from a place of ego.

While I was in that spiritual group, several couples chose celibacy as an act of redirecting their life-force toward God and made it their holy practice. The man's seed was to be considered and used for procreation only. While on one hand this would be deeply important for people who perhaps had too much party sex when young or misused their sexual life-force, it might be counterproductive for someone who needed to explore new through their bodies.

Of course, each person's path is different and sometimes because of this one can feel "othered" due to ideology.

A friend saw a naturopath who, through research and muscle testing, "prescribed" her an orgasm a day for better health. She lightheartedly shared this with her partner, who felt threatened and told others in our group. This led to dramatic fallout - she was called into a meeting with leadership, who criticized the naturopath's suggestion. What began as playful banter spiraled through gossip into a tense overreaction. I saw how something intimate could get twisted through multiple tellings, morphing into scandal instead of staying private. It taught me discernment about what to share, and when too much openness can backfire.

She was told, in a compassionate yet patronizing tone, "How awful that someone would tell you that. How wrong it was for someone to suggest you are sexually repressed." They lectured her that sexual energy is often misused and that she must transcend such inclinations.

When she sought to expand her understanding of sexuality, she faced gaslighting from someone who believed a yogic devotee should maintain purist detachment, dedicated to transcending worldly desires. Though it came from her best intentions, it was not actually supportive at the time.

In my own journey, I too encountered this gaslighting and shame, inflicted by those who deemed it necessary for a devoted spiritual seeker to confine herself to purist transcendence, suppressing all earthly explorations, including my sexuality. But I learned repression is not the path to wholeness or enlightenment.

What if instead we could merge heaven with Earth, rather than bring Earth to heaven and embody our spirituality and allow the fruit of the body to be good and part of our wholeness?

A few years later, I explored the mystic roots of Judaism and Kabbalah. This path viewed the body as a sacred vessel, finally allowing me to let go of spiritually exploiting myself.

This embodiment was even taken into prayer, where the movement was oftentimes rhythmic as if you were making love with the Creator in your devotion and praises. As a woman, I was honored with customs and songs each Friday night. In observant communities, a woman's hair and body are veiled, seen only by her husband. This modesty paired belonging with inner beauty, keeping feminine secrets for intimate times - vastly different from pop culture.

While I resisted being told to cover up, choosing my own style, over time I gained appreciation for modesty. My views continue to evolve, as I learn life's lessons around womanhood and the body. The jury remains out as this exploration continues.

Since beauty is found in things that can be seen but also in things that cannot, we'll dive deeper into beauty as a spiritual path. But, for now, I will say regarding modesty versus flaunting what you've got and revealing yourself as a sensual being, it is a very personal choice.

I will forever be proud of my breasts, which have fed my three sons and are a source of my female power, but I don't feel the need to share them visually any more. Again! A personal choice.

What I have learned in allowing for more modesty as I've aged is that the path of modesty isn't about shame and hiding our bodies, but is seen as beautiful because of the depth that comes with it; namely, it integrates the importance of both aspects – we are soul and we are body. It's not about being ashamed of what is underneath, but knowing it is valuable and that we have a right to guard it. Not everyone gets to look or touch it, as we recognize the power of the feminine body. We get to be true to ourselves and invite others to take a deeper look without flashing cleavage or upper thighs where the attention would go instead. It is our choice if we want to flash our flesh, or if we want to show that we are worthy of getting to know beyond the physical and outsides and instead access the unlimited beauty within us.

We have been culturally groomed and preened by male-dominated culture. But I will always love my long flowing hair and wearing makeup when I like. I still love playing dress-up and delighting in my inner femininity. I will reveal more about my path of beauty in Gateway 7.

I appreciate the groundedness in the culture of Judaism that has been an exploratory aspect on my spiritual path in the levels of being woman but not numbing it out with things like wearing neutrals, no-makeup, and baggy clothes, all of which I did for a time so I didn't have to be seen.

In certain spiritual communities, I began to find the pain points in the belief systems around being embodied and having an ego.

· There is a fear of embodiment because of the confusion that the body is not holy, and leads to disembodiment.

· There is even a flair of depersonalization disorder to be more awakened as you "lose" yourself in spirit.

· The ego is often seen as bad and therefore creates a lack of discernment and gaslighting because we aren't able to be overly sensitive, feel or express emotion, or have a differing of strong opinions; We are also seen as egotistical and not spiritual.

This all often works into "spiritual bypassing," to use spiritual beliefs to avoid our suffering or difficult feelings towards unresolved needs or personal obstacles.

This bypassing all plays into the transcendent way of rising above our mundane human lives to get past our pain and avoid the piece of being fully embodied. If we really do the work and feel our feelings, we can move mountains of grief that perhaps we may have stuffed into some deep corner of our childhoods and when we confront it we will have more energy and creativity. When we actually learn to have deeper awareness of our own feelings we can address, acknowledge and process them within our own spiritual practices so that we can fully learn their lessons and ultimately release them.

I have done that in repeated prayers where I am in intimate communion with the relational compassionate Divine One that is closer than your breath and more consistent in your life than your beating heart. You can literally be in inquiry and conversation as you process, forgive what needs to be forgiven and then fortify what wants to be solidified as you heal, transform, and clear the energy into newfound blessings and lifeforce in your being.

If you are spiritually bypassing to deal with life's more challenging curveballs, it makes it more difficult to step into a personal brand because you're walking around not fully rooted and not fully authentic in your psyche.

As it is said, the *only way out is through*, as I learned with my midwife's wisdom when giving birth to one of my sons.

Now, using suffering as our fuel for our transformation is not easy. Confronting the shadow, or hidden, parts in our psyche, is some of the hardest work we can do. This includes our terror at being visible which can stem from, and lead us to, a whole myriad of things to do the inner work around. When we do that work, however, there is "gold" for us to discover which liberates us into new realms of being. If we do not transmute our stuff, we will likely project it onto our most intimate relationships and people in our communities.

I have witnessed and journeyed through the shadow parts of both me and my clients who do not even want to be seen as a mystic or show up as a spiritual teacher for fears of current or past persecution. I have had multiple clients who had to confront something deep within the subconscious that identified with these past lives, where they were completely unsafe to show up in their power and magic or shine in their unique talents for fear of being burned at the stake, beheaded, crucified, or hung, et cetera.

If you feel shame or the need to hide your spirituality, you might be suffering from the "witch wound."

Yes, let's go there.

Rising from the Ashes of the Witch Wound

Grab your broom out of your inner closet because this is one of the deeper journeys I've explored with myself regarding visibility.

As mentioned above, we feel that deep subconscious or past-life wound when we are in our power, feel we have too many eyes on us, or share the outpouring of our unique gifts and our purpose.

If you've ever felt like you're holding back, or like you're not quite living up to your potential, it's possible that you have this wound. Sometimes called a "persecution imprint," this is a deep-seated belief that you are not safe while being too visible.

When I took myself through one of my own processes, I had a startling awakening that I often didn't like getting visible in my poetry, sharing my art, or simply a marketing message because it felt like...

DEATH.

I did some deep work around this, beginning with the awareness that it was there so I could continue to explore it and bring healing to it.

While I don't usually identify as a "witch" per se in this lifetime, I have distant memories of being accused as one – and sent to a torturous death – in a past life or lives.

As a young girl, I was blessed to have endless hours playing in the Pacific Northwest pastoral countryside with plentiful forests and abundance of plant life all around.

I would pretend I was a witch and mix up potent medicinal concoctions with sticky weeds, dank black soil, and bits of this-and-that to make the perfect elixir for whatever ailment was needed.

Then, in one particular past life regression in my early twenties, when I was dabbling in various paths to find my soul, I was told I had been a powerful herbalist and killed for my knowledge and experience.

Whatever may have been, I love hanging out in my artist studio and home-bodying up with a heavy helping of introversion.

During my healing journey, as I embrace the simple act of allowing my visibility to naturally fluctuate in the world, I find myself reflecting on the deep wounds that have been present from other times or present times. It becomes clear that much of it stems from the pervasive persecution imprint, where the instinct to keep something hidden and safeguarded takes hold.

One of these things in my life I have played with in this regard is my visibility. In this process, I am learning to release the shackles of fear and embrace the power of authenticity. I understand that true liberation lies in transcending the need to default to hiding and instead, courageously sharing my unique essence with the world when my soul is called. By doing so, I reclaim my inner strength and pave the way for others to embrace their own journey of self-discovery and empowerment.

A witch wound does not mean you necessarily were or are a witch, but is rather a deep-seated belief that you are not safe being too visible. This can be the result of past experiences where you were persecuted for being different.

Maybe you were teased for being too tall, or too skinny, or for wearing glasses. Maybe you were made to feel like an outsider because of your religion or your skin color. Maybe you can relate to that uneasy feeling but can't always pinpoint the origin.

Whatever the experience was, it left an imprint on your soul that said, "It's not safe to be seen."

A persecution imprint comes from past lives, when you may have been burned at the stake, tortured, or otherwise persecuted for your beliefs. These experiences can leave an energetic imprint that says, "Being seen is dangerous."

Only witches and heretics were burned alive (like Joan of Arc), with the assumption being that a charred body could not be raised on the "Day of Judgment".

Widowed ladies, single women, and other marginalized women were specifically targeted.

It's been said the trauma of these times have been ingrained in our ancestral DNA and passed through us generationally. These subconscious overlays still cause anxiety, guilt, shame regarding our spiritual gifts and being seen.

Both of these wounds can keep you from stepping into your power and living your fullest potential. As I write this, I still feel an empathetic sadness for all those whose lives were affected by these experiences and continue to carry the burden of these painful memories.

The good news is that there is a way to heal these very shadowy realms, more dark than a dark moon on Halloween.

The first step in healing your persecution imprint is to become aware of it.

Start paying attention to the ways in which you hold yourself back.

Do you avoid being in the spotlight? Do you downplay your achievements?

Do you find yourself apologizing frequently?

These are all signs that you may have a witch wound.

Once you've become aware of the ways in which these wounds are impacting your life, it's time to start working on healing them. There are many different techniques that can be effective, but some of our favorites include deep soul forgiveness work through prayer, energy work, and meditation.

Spend some time experimenting and find the techniques that work best for you.

And maybe you need to get a therapist or aligned coach or whatever you need to support you in the process of moving through subconscious shame.

Just remember, healing takes time and there is no "right" way to do it. Go at your own pace and trust that YOU ARE WORTHY OF HEALING.

My heartfelt hope is that you receive this message from the book, even if nothing else.

If you're ready to step into your power and live an abundant, fulfilling life, it's time to start healing your old witch wounds.

By becoming aware of the wound, doing your own inner work, and surrounding yourself with supportive people, you can begin to rewrite the story of your life and create a new reality for yourself.

It's time to step into your power and shine your light brightly in the world as the radiant holy being that you truly are!

I will remember the black sage healing tea, steeped in sunlight, that I would pour for my dolls and myself, and the mud thick between my toes as I played free in the thicket... just me, the spirit friends behind the veil, and all the forest critters watching.

I will remember and renew my INNOCENCE as it continues to reside across the lifetimes free from guilt and shame, like the purity of snow falling on a quiet winter's morning and the renewal of fire-sparks that rise toward the endless sky in search of becoming stars...

I will remember we are stardust, we are holy, and we are here.

And it's okay to do that thing... now.

We are safe, alive, and here to fully shine and be vibrant in this amazing life.

Witch on, bright cherry-cheeked sister.

We must deeply grieve these past persecutions and step into the time of the liberated spiritual entrepreneur.

The antidote is to step out of the old archetype of this tortured and victimized woman and into embracing our inner royalty.

Embodying the Empress archetype honors self-care, self-love, and the nurturing feminine essence. This transcends business, permeating all aspects of life with a holistic, life-giving approach. By adorning this archetype, we tap into the abundant wisdom and grace flowing through us, manifesting our highest potential.

You are a creator, a source from which all life has sprung. The Empress represents the desire within every living thing to grow and flourish. It represents the world bringing you forth, asking you to simply BE. The Empress personifies the impulse to nurture and be nourished as fertility and growth.

When we step into this space, we are not rattled about others' approval, but instead step into juicy creation, royal confidence, graceful manifestation, and sacred abundance. And soul-fueled visibility as you come to embody your brand. Anchoring in your brand contribution means aligning your actions, words, and intentions with the values and mission of your online presence. It means showing up with a sense of purpose and using your platform to create meaningful connections, inspire change, and spread your royal light as you are crowned by the Source of Blessings. Your authentic expression and genuine connection have the power to touch the lives of others, spark transformation, and create a ripple effect of multifaceted blessings.

One of my clients, Martha, reflected the shadow side of visibility when she was afraid to be seen and misinterpreted, like myself and so many of my clients have traversed and healed not just the persecution pieces but also the many levels of toxic shame of not feeling good enough to show up in the first place.

She said about our work together in supporting her to show up more visibly in her branding, her photos and online presence:

> *"Before we started working together, I was struggling*
> *with feeling scared to be visible on almost every*
> *level. I was scared to put my 'spiritual side' out to the*
> *world, but even more than that, I was scared to put*
> *my physical image out into the world, especially my*
> *pure, beautiful, soul self out to the world. I did not*
> *know that it was even possible to be seen and captured*
> *in my exact soul essence. I was scared of being*
> *misunderstood, not seen, not appreciated, not valued,*
> *and so forth." - Martha H.*

I now release the deep-seated fear stemming from puritanical religious dogma - the notion that the body is inherently bad or inferior to the holy spirit. I let go of the misguided view of the physical form as merely a disposable mortal shell, devoid of sacredness. I embrace my whole being, body and spirit, as holy and integrated.

This fear is that being fully embodied is "sinful" and personal branding is a commercial, superficial thing of only vanity. Many of my past clients have felt they would be seen as narcissistic if they show up embodied in their branding and social media presence.

I've personally worked through so many of these similar things. Yes, much of the time it feels more lovely to hang out in the spiritual realm where it is safe and all things are beautiful and the suffering of the worldly realms aren't present... like hanging out with my Magic Maple Tree.

Getting to the place where we can be visible is doing the inner work.

There is nothing supportive or holy about playing small and not shining out so others around you won't feel outshone or less secure of themselves. We must find freedom from our own shame and shit so that we can break free of the chains that hold us back in self-sacrifice and the prison of our own minds and fear.

In finding this freedom and acting upon it, we can activate and inspire others around us to do the same.

Creative Inspiration

Alongside the very inner spiritual aspect I had growing up was the wild, attention-loving girl, the inner rock star who just wanted to unleash her full expression in dance, singing, and wild creative fire for all to see and witness and ideally enjoy. The Cyndi Lauper classic "Girls Just Wanna Have Fun" comes immediately to mind, where she's calling us girls out to fulfill that need to step into our authentic, joyful selves. She calls out those boys who try to dim our light.

My grown woman self requires and desires both the spiritual being and the rock star. The integration makes me... myself. Just like it makes you, YOU.

Amazing to think about all the times when so young and free I would rip roar in seeking attention from family members and family friends by getting onto the stage. Before karaoke was a thing I would lip sync Madonna or MJ or Cyndi like nobody's business.

As a child, I wasn't afraid to shine.

What if we knew we were meant to just like we did then? Just as we forgot we have the ability to be creative and it is within ALL of us, it seems to be something we forget we have within us, like being bright and full of life.

You, beautiful soul, have a right to create.

As a little child, I imagine you danced and sang, finger painted wildly, made up silly nonsensical things and tried new adventures, built castles out of blankets and had elaborate tea parties with your stuffed animals.... and all without holding yourself back in fear or self-criticism.

You made things and created them because it was completely natural to your beingness, and because you experienced your inner and outer worlds through your senses as a way of exploring.

At some point on your journey into adulting, you let others tell you that it was nonsense (I was told to "simmer down"), and you learned to only do the things others said you were good at and walked away from things you were told weren't for you.

I'm deeply sorry for this, but you were lied to... it's not right... because we are all creative in so many ways.

If it feels good to create, just do it. There is no harm in playing if it makes you feel vibrant and alive.

Creativity is the order of the Universe.

If you feel inspired to make music, fling paint, write, wear that flamboyant acid green and hot pink dress out on the town, craft, or move your body in unique ways, remember that it is your *birthright*. Say *heck yes* to your creative impulses that fuel your heart and soul and express yourself freely, for creativity is an inherent part of who you are.

Where did the "not good enough" voice even come from? Who says that? It doesn't even have to be good enough because that's a subjective measuring device. If you make a mistake in your art, do it anyway. Keep going. It's about the ecstasy in the expression and in the transmutation of the healing.

It's the heart of what makes creating necessary.

So make something... do something... create something.

Your creative wild self awaits you now, and you have *full permission.*

When we shine, we can inspire, give permission, and remind others to do the same, and this in itself is a true blessing.

So much of shine allows your unique creativity to come forth.

Let's contemplate that, and the inspiration of how to create and the connections between our creative life and spiritual life as we begin this journey of Holy Hot Visibility.

The first thing to realize is we are ALL creative beings. Whether you think you are boring or not, everyone has the capacity for creativity.

Consider some of the oldest cultures on Earth, and how the arts were part of the tapestry of everyday life. All the people in the community would take place in the rituals involving song, dance, and painting – either their bodies or the walls. Creativity was not reserved for the artists or a special talent in the tribe, but for everyone.

We each can give ourselves permission to be makers. Not because it has to feel special or important or even original, but because we are here to be creators, because we have an innate need to. And what if a lot of our desire to bring creativity out into the world is so other people can see it? That is the equation of the visibility piece we will get to. But the creative flow is a currency, a Divine spark, that is birthed from the internal realm of our psyche, our heart, our soul.

Since creation *is* essential for your wellbeing, let's talk about some ways to get inspired.

I've realized lately that my painting and all my entrepreneurial endeavors is literally my soul's way of inner alchemy and transmuting emotion, helping embody archetypes and energies that I create, clearing out the stuff from the past, and also coming into alignment with where I am headed.

It heals and transmutes. It transforms me bit by bit. I've thought about some of the practices I've taken on over the years to allow me to feel that internal spark my soul longs for.

The first thing is about mindset and getting intentional with what I want to attune to within and create. This journey is rooted in the power of affirmation, decisive action, and unwavering commitment to oneself and others in pursuit of our desires. It is crucial to recognize and overcome the tendency to passively linger in a state of uncertainty, be it in choosing what to create or which course to embark upon. Such indecision can become a self-sabotaging trap that hinders progress. Instead, let us firmly make up our minds and embrace the courage to make definitive decisions, propelling ourselves forward from the realms of confusion into the realm of purposeful action.

There can be the "I don't know what I want to create or paint or I don't know what course I want to create..." That is just a passive, self-sabotage way of not moving forward and staying in confusion. So make up your mind to make a decision.

Declare what you are going to do in your art or creative process, whether it be trying a new mixed media technique, sitting down to write free-flow for twenty minutes, or just dancing for ten minutes straight to move the energy.

I find clarity a recurring theme in moving forward with showing up in the first place.

How you dive into your creative process is important too. Once you get your music on, you'll get in the flow.

So when I start art, I usually do a few things.

√ Make a cup of tea

√ Start up the music

√ With the tea, tune into what might unfold unless I'm continuing on a current project

√ Check in with feelings and moods

√ Think about what type of art or creative project would suit me

√ Big brushes and messy paints for wilder music. Or, maybe a podcast if I'm feeling a bit slower and want to take my time and meander a bit.

It's about honoring the unfolding creative energy and embodying its unique expression through your art.

When inspiration strikes, it's like a rising fire demanding release. My brushes dance wildly across the canvas or my fingers feverishly type, channeling the creative spark into art.

But where does that original spark originate?

There's me - my mindset and my body. And plenty of obstacles, such as lack of inspiration, lack of time, clutter, energy at any given time of day, perfectionism, self-doubt, and so on.

The only way through these obstacles is to be resolute about what you are determined to create. From that point forward, you commit to taking inspired action and embracing the challenges as opportunities for growth.

With soul-fueled determination, you embark on the journey of manifesting your vision and bringing it to fruition. You rise above the noise of self-doubt or fear, knowing that you have the power within you to overcome the prickly obstacles and achieve the sacred success you desire.

Creative Self-Expression Radiance Ritual

Materials Needed
· Journal or notebook
· Art supplies (paint, markers, colored pencils, etc.)
· Music playlist
· Sacred space (a quiet and comfortable area where you can focus)

1. Prepare Your Space
Find a quiet and comfortable space where you can create without distractions. Set up your art supplies, journal, and any other items you feel called to use during the ritual. Create an ambiance that supports your creative flow. Light candles, burn incense, or play calming music to set the mood.

2. Grounding and Centering

Take a few deep breaths to center yourself. Close your eyes and visualize roots growing from the soles of your feet, connecting you to the Earth's energy. Feel yourself grounding and becoming present in the moment.

3. Setting Intentions

Open your journal and write down your intentions for this ritual. What qualities or aspects of yourself do you want to express and enhance? How do you want to cultivate magnetism in your life? Be clear and specific with your intentions, focusing on the feelings and experiences you desire.

4. Freeform Expression

Begin playing your chosen music playlist. Let the rhythm and melodies guide your creative flow. Pick up your art supplies and start expressing yourself freely on the blank canvas or paper. Allow your intuition to guide your brushstrokes, color choices, and shapes. Don't worry about creating something perfect— this is about letting your inner essence come alive.

Let go of any expectations or self-judgment. Embrace the process of self-expression and enjoy the freedom of creating without constraints. Take some time and space with this.

5. Reflect and Release

Take a moment to sit with your artwork. Observe the colors, shapes, and energy it holds. What messages or emotions arise for you as you observe it?

Open your journal and write down any insights, reflections, or feelings that emerged during the creative process. Use this space to explore your thoughts and deepen your self-awareness.

6. Integration and Affirmations

Close your ritual by affirming your intentions and embracing your authentic magnetism. Speak aloud affirmations that resonate with your desires and the qualities you wish to embody. Repeat these affirmations with conviction, believing in your own inherent beauty, authenticity, and magnetism.

7. Gratitude and Closing

Give thanks for the chance to interact with your authentic self and cultivate magnetism through creative self-expression.

Take a few final deep breaths, feeling a sense of grounding and alignment with your intentions. Blow out any candles, put out your incense, and tidy up your space, infusing it with gratitude and positivity as you create sacred closure.

Remember that creative self-expression is a deeply personal journey of self-discovery. It's all about finding what works best for you and adapting it to your own preferences and needs. The gem here is to make it a regular practice to continue nurturing your magnetism and honoring your unique creative self-expression as holy.

So, go ahead and dive into this ritual whenever you feel the desire to tap into your natural magnetism and unleash your essence. Set aside dedicated time for yourself, create sacred space where you feel comfortable and inspired, and let your intuition guide you. Explore different forms of self-expression that resonate with you, whether it's through art, writing, movement, or any other medium that sparks your creativity.

And as always, allow yourself to let go of any expectations or judgments. Self-led ritual is about connecting with your inner truth and expressing yourself freely, without seeking approval or validation from others, so dance wildly in the joy of self-discovery and playfulness as you explore new ways to express your most intimate part of yourself! Your confidence will grow, and your magnetism will radiate naturally and aligned with your deepest desires.

Your Path Through the Second Gateway

In the realm of online visibility, embracing creativity is essential to stand out and connect with your audience in a meaningful way. The Second Gateway encourages you to tap into your unique creative gifts and express them authentically. Here are a few ways to play with this energy as you allow your Second Gateway to bloom.

1. **Explore different content formats.** Allow yourself to explore different mediums, whether it's through writing, visuals, videos, or other forms of content creation. Experiment with different content formats that allow you to express your creativity. Consider writing engaging blog posts, creating visually captivating graphics or videos, recording podcasts, or even hosting live streams. Find the medium that resonates with you and enables you to share your message authentically.

2. **Tap into your Passion.** Discover what truly ignites it and infuse it into your online presence. Align your content with topics and themes that genuinely excite and turn you on. When you're passionate about what you're sharing, that energy shines through so that even words we use every day have a vibrant and magnetic quality that captivate your dream audience in an entirely new way.

3. **Authentic self-expression lies at the core of establishing a genuine connection with your audience.** The second Gateway

calls you to embrace your true self, free from the constraints of comparison or societal expectations, so trust your creative impulses and let your true essence shine through. Share your stories, experiences, and insights with honesty and transparency. By doing so, you inspire others to do the same and create an environment of trust and authenticity.

4. **Embrace the ecstatic joy of creative exploration and allow it to flow effortlessly into your online visibility journey.** Play with cultivating creative ritual and set aside dedicated time for nurturing your creativity. Create a ritual that allows you to tap into your creative flow, be it through journaling, sketching, or engaging in other creative practices. This dedicated time will help you access your authentic self-expression and bring fresh ideas to your online visibility.

Remember, the journey of awakening the Second Gateway is an ongoing process. Nurture your creativity, continuously seek inspiration, and allow yourself the freedom to evolve and grow organically.

As we move forward to the next gateway, remember to honor yourself for the courage to be seen in this way. By doing so, you pave the way for a captivating and soulful online visibility that leaves a lasting impact on you and creates a ripple effect of inspiration for your audience.

2nd Gateway Journal Prompts

1. Take a moment to think about the activities or hobbies that truly ignite your passion and creativity. How can you infuse these passions into your brand. How you express yourself? How can you use them to create an joyful connection, with your audience?

2. Explore the role of joy in shaping your brand and gaining visibility. What brings you happiness and joy? How can you incorporate these elements into your brands messaging, visuals and overall experience to make an impact that uplifts others?

3. For the ladies, reflect on the qualities and strengths associated with femininity within yourself. How can you. Embody these qualities in your brands visibility efforts? In what ways can you celebrate femininity through the expression of your brand?

4. Dive deep into understanding your process. How do you. Cultivate your creativity? What practices or rituals do you engage in to support the flow of your ideas? How can these practices become a part of your brands foundation and expression?

5. Consider the impact that you want to have on others through your pursuits and personal brand. How do you envision making people feel when they interact with your brand? In what ways can you utilize your creativity and personal expression to uplift inspire. Evoke emotions, in others?

RADIANT CONFIDENCE

Insignificant to Significant

Self-Worth, Self-Belief, Personal Power

"Do you have the courage to bring forth the treasures that are hidden within you?" ~ Elizabeth Gilbert

Confidence is actually a choice. When I began to understand that, I was blown away.

Claiming your own flavor of creative brilliance and owning it can be a pathway into allowing for more Holy Hot Visibility in your world.

How and when do we realize and give ourselves permission to be just that?

This is when we activate our center of power, or solar plexus chakra, that resides just above our navel and is connected to our kundalini.

In martial arts, particularly practices like Qigong and Tai Chi, the "Dantian" concept holds significant importance. It's regarded as the powerful grounding force that initiates all movements. The lower Dantian, located a few inches below the navel, aligns closely with the region of the solar plexus chakra.

In Reiki, an energy healing technique from Japan, the solar plexus chakra finds resonance with the "Hara." This energetic center, situated below the navel, is considered a wellspring of both physical and spiritual energy, providing a vital source of life force.

Additionally, in certain interpretations, the solar plexus region in Ancient Egyptian spirituality correlates with the notion of a "solar center." This center is deemed essential for energy flow and acts as a conduit to higher consciousness. These concepts underline the universality of recognizing significant energy centers within the body across various spiritual and holistic practices.

Wherever your "sun-in-our-belly" resides, it serves as the center of your aura, the source of light, magnetism, and profound confidence (power). This inner radiance can be accessed as needed, especially when displaying our brilliance while building or upleveling a website or personal brand. It takes tremendous courage to shine and be seen in all our glory, but tapping into this inner source empowers us in our visibility with grace and authenticity.

Every individual possesses one or several "boulders" that can hinder our efforts to become more visible or assert ourselves in different situations. Just know that defining your personal brand doesn't have to be so hard. It can simply be you being you, from your enlightened perspective, and boldly sharing it in the world.

Here are some of the common ways we self-sabotage ourselves in being visible in our brands:

- Self-consciousness and imposter syndrome about your value stop you from launching or getting visible.

- You are living with the feeling that everyone else has it figured out but you.

- When you know what makes you different and amazing in the eyes of your ideal client, but you don't know how to communicate it to them.

- Spinning around with your Muse and too many good ideas or being stuck in the "creative lab" because you don't know where to focus.

- Working for your clients 24/7 instead of growing your own biz and being visible.

I've also observed three primary common hurdles that my clients encounter, along with strategies to overcome them, ultimately leading to greater life satisfaction, attracting more clients, and achieving financial prosperity, among other benefits. I have included the main three categories in the following pages...

3 Main Visibility Obstacles and Their Antidotes

1. Overcoming Criticism & Rejection

We can be so afraid of others not liking our work, our creativity, our offering... part of our soul. We can also feel triggered by rejection at varying degrees, depending on who it is that is doing the criticizing or rejecting and what that person – or the respect we hold for them – means to us.

A big example of this is women's body consciousness around being seen in their photoshoots. When a woman feels overweight, or has some other image issue, I'll often hear, "I'll just do it after I lose just ten or fifteen more pounds," et cetera. This is what happened when Stephanie Dawn and I were discussing her upcoming personal brand photoshoot. I supported her in moving through her desire to be at her ideal weight, helped her realize that the time was now, and that the photos would support her in feeling beautiful and radiant in the next level in her business success and prosperity. And they did just that. She was ready for a massive uplevel in her business and ultimately decided not to allow her body awareness to stop her from moving forward. *Psssst – as if being taken seriously as a business coach has ANYTHING to do with having some extra weight on!*

Here is what she had to say about the experience:

> *"I was indeed the heaviest I had been since being pregnant. What happened was this: my need/desire to up level was greater than my upset around being photographed at my heaviest. I knew the time was now and ultimately, I was right. I am so glad I went for it." – Stephanie Dawn, Sacred Business Coach*

Antidote Magic to Judgment and Criticism

First, it is important to briefly acknowledge the emotions that another has triggered within you so you can move through it, forgive yourself for buying into a false story, and silently forgive another for what they have projected upon you. View being pushed to your limits as an opportunity to move beyond them.

Treat yourself with compassion, place your hand over your heart, and call on the Divine that is right within you to affirm your worthiness of success at a soul level. Refuse to let rejection define you.

We must maintain perseverance in the heart and mind – and not make spacious generalizations – if we run into rejection. If someone criticizes your writing, okay, it's just not their cup of tea. If a potential lover rejects you, don't find yourself to be unlovable but instead know that the Divine has a much vaster purpose for you and there is great abundance in the world to be enjoyed and experienced in life.

2. Becoming your Own Expert

"When you're an artist," wrote best-selling author, musician, and artist Amanda Palmer, "nobody ever tells you or hits you with the magic wand of legitimacy. You have to hit your own head with your own handmade wand."

In other words, unless you can be fully expressed you feel like a little bit of a fraud, teaching these things but not actually doing them. If you're an entrepreneur, you need to be walking your talk.

Obliterating the Fraud Factor

The "Fraud Factor" emerges when doubt creeps in, causing us to question the value we bring to clients, customers, or audiences. This phenomenon often arises when we are new to our ventures, but it can also sneak in as we transition into higher levels of success and greater abundance, leading us to believe that we need more credentials or additional degrees. Many of us grapple with the desire to feel secure and grounded in what we already know, drawing from our accumulated knowledge and experiences in this lifetime or even from past lives. It is when we step beyond the boundaries of our familiar comfort zone that we may find ourselves questioning our own identity and what unique contributions we have to offer to the world.

We can focus on self-doubt and get in our heads around how little we feel we know, or how much more we "should" glean before we can really offer more value. Or, we can dig into the wealth of knowledge that we already possess. One example is when women coaches go to change their structure from a per-session offering to larger packages (i.e. a three-month commitment); they often don't feel in alignment with this jump, even though packing it up this way is much more effective and transformational for their clients and more lucrative for them.

When I created a larger package for my website clients, it was the most potent combination of all my offerings from brand archetypes, visual branding, brand mentoring and business coaching, and website design and development. Though I continued to do one-off services, that was a "big value" that upleveled my offerings in a way that was much more impactful for clients than a logo here or a book cover there.

Antidote Magic to the Fraud Factor

There is only one of you, so embrace your uniqueness. Submit to the sovereignty of your inner expert. Remember, you are a teacher to those who need you!

Obliterating the Fraud Factor is to focus on what you know to increase your personal and soul value. This is about life experience and the innate wisdom that is already within you. We tend to downplay our knowledge; we think others already know it because it is so obvious to us. But the amazing thing is that there is *no one* who teaches the way we do; our unique set of stories, our personalities, and offerings is totally genuine and authentic to our own being! We are each so lusciously alive in our own makeup that when we are fully ourselves, perfect in the moment and on the phase of our paths and evolution (and OWNING IT) people will be attracted to who we are. It is often surprising to discover that others may perceive us with more confidence and allure than we see in ourselves.

A wild realization, isn't it?

By allowing ourselves to step into leadership and set an example, we unlock a valuable gem of wisdom: getting out of our own way. When we remove self-imposed obstacles, we create an environment that makes it effortless for those who desire what we have to offer to connect with us. In doing so, we radiate with the luminosity of our own abundance and unique qualities, attracting others and creating a harmonious flow of energy and opportunities.

3. Moving Beyond the Fear to Shine

It's not uncommon to feel a fear of shining brightly. We may have encountered situations where others felt insecure or intimidated by our beauty and radiance, leading us to believe that we should dim our light to make them more comfortable. But in doing so, we deny ourselves the opportunity to fully express our authentic selves and share our unique gifts with the world.

It's important to recognize that our shine is not meant to diminish others, but rather to inspire and uplift them. By embracing our own brilliance, we give permission for others to do the same, creating a ripple effect of empowerment and transformation.

We can try to hide our light to try and prevent others from feeling insecure or smaller than us. Sometimes we've had experiences with others being afraid of our beauty or radiance, and we've tried to dim it down.

Or, we've felt the vastness of our soul, and the divinity of our spirit beyond the soul, personality, and all things, and we tried to rein it in because it felt too immense.

Dumbing or numbing ourselves down is not doing anyone any favors, as we are all here to lead by example, and ideally to shine and spread the light.

It is our birthright to be gorgeous, talented, successful, brilliant, and to shine like the light striking a diamond. We had an innate knowing of this as little children, before the perceived oppression of society, our upbringing, and others' opinions, projections, and spells upon us.

When we reconnect to that childlike mindset, we free ourselves from the perceived limits of the physical plane, and expand into infinite potentiality which encompasses prosperity, health, wealth, and spiritual power.

So let's let go of the fear and allow your light to shine with unapologetic radiance, knowing that it has the power to ignite the flames of possibility in others.

Antidote Magic to Moving Beyond the Fear to Shine

So, how do we do "allow ourselves to shine"? The term sounds so simple and it is often overused. And it's not like we are metallic or a body of water with the sun bouncing off us, creating a reflection that makes us shine like the moon. The shine comes from a place of serenity and self-love inside; it radially expands outward into the world, but it is always sourced from the connection to the Oneness of Divinity that quietly resides within us.

It involves shifting our perspective and reframing our beliefs about ourselves and our place in the world. Instead of allowing fear to hold us back, we can choose courage and step into our power.

Tapping into this is a practice, and it is the only sustainable way to stand in our most sovereign selves.

When we can realize it's not about the fear of failure, but more the fear of success, we can start working with this illusion.

Because, in truth, that's what our greatest fear is: SUCCESS.

That means we are powerful, abundant, and moving into and receiving everything our heart desires. It's moving beyond any self-worth issues, and allowing all our past failures to fall by the wayside so we can step into a life of miracles and creating heaven around us.

We can step into this realm of more success by, first, deciding we are going to be that, then releasing excuses and blocks that we have put in our way. How do we release them? Say a prayer calling on the angels to take you to the next level, write it big in the sand, journal, dance... whatever it takes for you to banish your visibility obstacles.

We can take time to explore the roots of the fear. What stories or past experiences have contributed to this fear of shining? By gaining awareness, you can begin to challenge and release these limiting beliefs.

We can celebrate the individuality and the qualities that make you special. Recognize that your unique essence is a gift to be shared with the world that innocent part of your deepest self that allows you to shine authentically.

Please be gentle with yourself as you navigate this journey and understand that it's natural to have moments of doubt or insecurity. As you practice self-compassion and remind yourself that you are worthy of success, visibility, and recognition, you will become more embodying in your inherent birthright of shining radiance.

You might also look for a group of like-minded individuals who will encourage, support, and celebrate your growth while giving you a place to shine. Just practice your *heck no* to the online trolls and toxic people in your life.

Take that inspired action to step aside from your comfort zone and take small, intentional steps toward visibility. This could include sharing your voice through social media, offering your expertise in your field, or participating in networking events. Each action will build momentum and strengthens confidence.

Remember, the fear to shine is merely an illusion that holds us back from fully embracing our true potential. By acknowledging and challenging this fear, we open ourselves up to a world of infinite possibilities.

Find what works, keep practicing that, and you will discover a whole new sense of freedom and joy in the spaciousness you find when those blocks disappear.

When we spread our wings to soar and allow for this liberation, we automatically transmit this potential upon others and allow it to flow into our lives more.

Where are you stopping yourself?

You are a treasured creation of the Divine. Holding back your greatness serves no one's benefit. There is no wisdom in diminishing yourself to spare others from feeling insecure when you're around. Just like innocent children, we are all meant to exude radiant presence.

Our purpose is to bring forth the Divine splendor that resides within us. This potential isn't for a select few... it dwells within each and every one of us. By allowing our own self-worth to shine, we can inspire others to do the same.

So dearest, embrace your light, step into your power, and rediscover yourself shining more brightly in all areas of your life.

The world is waiting for your brilliance.

Embrace Your Inner Queen

One late afternoon, at the dog-friendly end of the beach, two ladies walked toward me, a small wiry furball bounding around them.

"What kind of dog is that?" I asked.

The woman facing me turned toward her friend. "I dunno, what is it?"

The other woman turned toward me as we passed each other, walking backward and in opposite directions.

"She's a _____ terrier," she replied.

I didn't catch the other word because when she looked at me there was this weird familiarity.

She could see that what she said didn't fully register. Instead, there was this vast pause unfolding as I was looking into or beyond her... and she slowly offered me a beautiful, enchanting smile.

She recognized me, recognizing her.

It was Natalie Portman, one of the few actors I have really admired in movies. At the time, I was living in Santa Barbara, north of the Hollywood area and had run into my share of celebs, but there was something in this moment that was different.

There was a gift. A transmission, of sorts. And a simple camaraderie.

"Thanks," I responded as we each smiled at each other, turned forward in our respective directions, and carried forth on our individual paths.

Then I turned to my son and friend and quietly exclaimed, "That was the Princess Leia of the new *Star Wars* movies!" My teenager quickly corrected me, saying her name was *not* Princess Leia. Later, I remembered her as Queen Padmé Amidala.

The colorful, rich, and adventurous life I imagined she experiences flashed before me. And she seemed happy as a new mamma slowly strolling the beach.

The point of this story is not what character she played or even how beautiful she was, but this spark of I SEE YOU TOO.

This recognition of Queen to Queen. Woman to Woman. Soul to Soul.

There was no hierarchy. Just potential. And just some reminder that success or whatever we desire is here for us.

And this spark in her owning her glamour, beauty, fame, and total willingness and ability to be seen.

She saw me seeing her, and she saw me back. Sisters in this moment in time... messy hair blowing in the wind and our children at our sides.

As brief as it was, a lot was transferred in that moment, and I wanted to share what I gleaned with you.

How Natalie Portman Taught Me 3 Valuable Things in 10 Seconds

1. It's time to be great and allow yourself to be seen in that. Let your dignity come through. Want to go big? Time to stop thinking small. Aren't feeling it? *Fake it 'til you make it.* Follow your goals. Manifest your personal iconic brand. Uplevel your life, your business, your dream, your trajectory.

2. The moment has arrived to embrace your own glamour. Draw it down from the realms beyond and infuse it into your very being. Inhale its essence, from the pinnacle of your head to the extremities of your toes. Glamour and opulence aren't exclusive to Hollywood celebrities; they are within your grasp as well.

Yet, keep in mind that the true essence of glamour emanates from the radiance and joy of your soul; from the wellspring of your innate feminine mystique.

Women, permit the innate beauty bestowed upon you by the Divine to captivate the world as well. The rose was never intended to be ordinary or dull, was it? That doesn't beckon the honeybee. The rose simply exists, radiant and enchanting, as she is.

Claim your queendom with new grace-imbued confidence. Revel in your sovereignty, establish boundaries, wield your power, and shine as a guiding light.

Embody your glamourous being with imagery and essence that could be as luscious as any celebrity may have it. And add your big splash of soul and prismatic shine.

3. It's time to SHINE. SHINE. SHINE. It's okay if they can't handle your light; hand 'em a pair of shades if you want. Let it go. Your natural radiance isn't here to slow you down or give you a shadow to hide in. Come out from the visibility closet and let's light up the world together. Or if you're an entrepreneur, at least we can start with the online world.

Perhaps any of us will get the chance to activate someone's potential with a simple smile.

Remember that when we embrace our significance, the radial self-worth expands into the world without even having to take from our own source. It just is.

Your Path Through the Third Gateway

As you reach the culmination of the Third Gateway and bring its learning into the world, you will see that significance is here to ignite your personal power and confident leadership in your online visibility.

This leads to stepping into your authority to make a luminous impact.

Here are a few practices to help you harness your personal power and confidently lead in your visibility:

Cultivate self-confidence by learning to believe in yourself and your abilities. Build self-confidence through self-reflection, acknowledging your accomplishments, and celebrating your strengths. Recognize that you have valuable insights and experiences to offer, and that your voice deserves to be heard. And finally, embody a self-assured presence in your online visibility as you keep persevering with this practice, inspiring others to trust and follow your lead and gaining the momentum of believing in yourself as you go.

Develop thought leadership as you position yourself as a thought leader in your lasered-in industry by consistently sharing valuable and insightful, inspired content that lights you up. Offer unique perspectives, innovative soul-fueled ideas, and actionable strategies that resonate with the hearts of your audience. Be proactive in staying up to date with industry trends and developments, positioning yourself as a go-to resource for valuable information and guidance

Lead with that beautiful, aligned authenticity. I can't state this enough: this is the cornerstone of effective and soulful leadership. Be gorgeously genuine, transparent, and true to yourself in all your online interactions and connect with your audience on a personal level, sharing stories and experiences that highlight your authenticity. By leading with authenticity, you inspire trust and deeper connections with your community.

True confidence stems from embracing vulnerability and being comfortable with being seen as imperfect; for gosh sakes, we are human, not gods! Understand that it's okay to make mistakes or face challenges along the way. Embrace vulnerability as an opportunity for growth and all the learning, because when you allow yourself to be vulnerable you become more authentic and relatable to your people, building trust and confidence in your online presence.

Take some time to acknowledge and celebrate your accomplishments, whether that means stepping out to be just a little more vulnerable or showing up live on social media! No matter how small those wins may seem, recognize your progress and the steps you've taken toward your goals, because praising the wins boosts your confidence and reinforces a positive inner mindset. You can even be so brave as to share your achievements with your audience or community to inspire and motivate others while reinforcing your own self-belief.

Remember, confidence is a journey, and it can be cultivated and strengthened over time. By embracing vulnerability, popping the confetti over the wins, and practicing self-compassion, you'll gradually build a solid foundation of confidence that will radiate through your online visibility.

Kindling collaborative relationships as you recognize the power of connection that we are diving into in the next Gateway and the collective wisdom that comes from working with others. Seek opportunities to collaborate with like-minded individuals, influencers, and experts in your field or niche. By nurturing collaborative relationships, you not only expand your reach but also cultivate a community of supporters who amplify and share your message.

By harnessing your personal power and embracing your true significance as a part of confident leadership in your online visibility, you have the opportunity to significantly impact the lives of your audience.

Embody this aligned and authentic authority, share your insights with conviction, and lead by example. As you step into this elevated space, you'll attract and grow your dream audience and create a lasting impact that extends well beyond the online realm.

3rd Gateway Journal Prompts

1. Take a moment to think about times, in your life when you felt like you didn't matter and how it affected your self confidence. How can you tap into the energy of your third gateway to overcome these feelings of insignificance and become a leader in your life and personal brand?

2. Explore the idea of confidence and its connection to how visible you're in your brand. How can you project confidence through the messages, visuals and interactions of your brand? How does this confidence contribute to the empowerment and success of your brand?

3. Ponder on your strengths and talents. How can you utilize these qualities to establish yourself as a leader in your field and within your brand? In what ways can you use these strengths to inspire and empower others?

4. Contemplate on the concept of radiance and its relevance, to the visibility of your brand. How can you let your true self shine brightly through the expression of your brand? How does this radiance. Connect with the audience you want to reach?

5. Take some time to reflect on any fears or doubts that might be holding you back from embracing visibility and stepping into your power. What strategies can help you overcome these fears building a sense of self belief, empowerment within yourself but for showcasing it through your personal brand?

Part Two

Transforming

.

GATEWAY 4:

HEART-CENTEREDNESS

Disconnected to Connected

Service, Balance, Attunement

"Work with your heart, because – I promise – if you show up for your work day after day after after day you just might get lucky enough some random morning to burst right into bloom."
— *Elizabeth Gilbert, Big Magic: Creative Living Beyond Fear*

Want to touch divinity? The authenticity of this life? Let's journey beyond the ego that separates and compares us to all things or any thing. When we trust and love ourselves with compassion and it becomes a more integrated part of our experience, there is a harmony we nurture between the head and the heart.

It's no secret that the world of online visibility can be a minefield. Navigating the waters of social media, client work, and video can be a daunting task. However, there is one very important thing that you can do to ensure that your journey is a successful one: connect with your heart by opening and balancing your heart chakra.

As mentioned earlier, the is associated with love, compassion, and connection, as well as the element of air. It governs our ability to love ourselves and others, and to give and receive love unconditionally. When this chakra is in balance, we feel confident and connected to our authentic selves. We are able to radiate compassion, kindness, and love. We are also able to step into our power and visibility with ease. However, when it is out of balance, we may feel lonely, disconnected, anxious, or even ashamed. We may also find it difficult to be seen and heard by others.

There are several ways to open and balance your heart chakra.

Create a Visibility Plan to Support Your Heart-Centered Business

If you want to create a Visibility Plan that feels good to you and supports your heart-centered business, it is essential that you take the time to connect with your heart first.

Here are some ways to do that:

• **Meditate:** Spend at least five minutes each day meditating on your heart chakra. Visualize a green light shining from your chest and breathe into the sensation of love and compassion.

• **Journal:** Write about what it means for you to live and work from your heart. How does that look in your business? What type of clients would you like to attract? How can you show up more authentically on social media?

• **Chant:** Chanting or singing can be a powerful way to connect with your heart chakra. Try chanting "om" or "ah" for a few minutes each day, or find a song that resonates with you and sing it at the top of your lungs!

• **Get Physical:** Exercise is also a great way to get in touch with your heart. Taking a brisk walk outdoors or doing some heart-opening yoga poses can help you to connect with your body and open up your heart chakra.

By taking the time to connect with your heart before you start reaching out and getting visible online, you will be laying the foundation for a more authentic, successful, and heart-centered journey into visibility.

Let's move beyond the incessant internal dialogue of the mind and arrive in a state of open-hearted presence connected to our pure self. We can make the empowered choice to release the need to be approved of, the need to be in control of how the outward affects us, and the need to judge ourselves or others. Releasing more needs around the convoluted stories in our heads is the game-changer. Notice when these things come up, call them out for what they are, and then move on into the ecstasy that resides beyond illusionary thinking. Then go spread your message wide and far from this humbled, empowered, authentic space.

When we hold close our inner heart, we become our own temple, we only need to close our eyes and breathe in the source of the Divine energy running through our chakras. This is the origin of our power and the lifeforce that fuels our being. Once we realize what we are made out of, we cannot help but to choose the path of a spiritual life.

Healing the past around our spiritual truth and reconnecting to what is real for us with our connection to our own self, others, and our Creator is getting to the heart of the matter.

Some religions promise heaven in the afterlife, after a journey of good choices and deeds. However, I've known in my heart since a young age that we are here to understand heaven here on Earth. What we chose as our spiritual practice is the doorway to get there. When we commit to a spiritual life, we often choose to integrate that into all aspects of our lives and, yes, our business.

We can play with the embodiment of dance, make time for stillness and meditation, pray out loud, and bring in the highest intentions into our business. We get to cultivate the ability to access our inner happy spiritual place in the stretches and challenging moments.

How to integrate more of the holy aspect of your wholeness into your daily world and business?

1. Embrace your feelings – even challenging ones

It starts with awareness and acknowledgment. Having feelings is part of being human and understanding them is necessary and good self-care. To connect deeply with ourselves, we can't just spiritually bypass our feelings, avoid them, or numb them out with overeating, drinking, codependency, or a plethora of other vices to escape. It goes the same for our businesses – we can cultivate a great deal of awareness around whether to show up or not show up when we are attuned with how we are feeling, and the undercurrent of fear or insecurity, so we can shift obstacles as needed. Allow yourself space and acceptance to express and move through whatever is real in any moment, and get to that space of authentic wholeness in all aspects of life. Attune to a daily morning spiritual practice to get your mindset revved up and aligned for your entire day as an anchor in your business, parenting, and life.

2. Turn off the screens and distractions and find yourself.

If you're focusing or obsessing on what everyone else in the industry is doing, you may get mired in the quicksand of comparison, which brings a whole other boatload of unwanted distractions from where you need and want to go. Cut down your time on social media unless you are using it for business and marketing and get in the reality of real-time and real people. Be with your family, take a walk in nature (and leave your phone behind), laugh with friends like you're back in high school, and let loose more in areas of life that require it.

Give yourself permission to dismiss any comparisons between the messy, creative, and wild reality of your own life and the seemingly flawless facade presented on another person's curated Instagram reel. Allow yourself to let go of the need to measure up to an idealized version of someone else's life. Instead, embrace the authenticity and uniqueness of your own journey, celebrating the beauty that arises from embracing imperfections and the unpredictable nature of life's twists and turns. As you may know, most of what is amazing in life is not photoshopped, curated, or filtered.

3. Bring playfulness into your spirituality

A good friend of mine who initiates women into an ordained priestesshood recently took me to a birthday dinner of Mexican food. There we were in the open-air seating area, sipping mango margaritas, and hooting and hollering as she described her entry-level initiates. We can be so serious as we try to find the Divine with all that single-minded focus on our pituitary gland in meditation, saying a certain amount of mantras, and the very real pleading for our sins to be cleared and for us to be spared the judgments of some bearded guy in the sky.

Many of us who grew up going to temple or Sunday School distanced ourselves from spirituality because, well, it was boring! But when you let spirituality become a creative outlet infused with play it's a whole other gig.

In the beginning of my journey along a path—connecting to consciousness through the beauty of the earth elements—I immersed myself in the world of crystals. Their captivating beauty served as a conduit to infuse vitality into the energy that enveloped my surroundings.

When it comes to your business, consider placing a candle infused with an essential oil that resonates with abundance, while writing a symbolic check for your desired annual income. Crown it with a citrine crystal as a constant reminder of prosperity and triumph. This practice is essential to fully embody your intention.

Speak out loud your gratitude that you are wealthy in the arms of your Creator. You are blessed with so much and are a lively, rich aspect of the abundance of creation.

Try out various things and make it fun and make it your own.

The most essential thing you can do is to follow your inner voice to create a relationship with the Divine that is authentically you and hold all aspects of your life as a spiritual being, including your entrepreneurial endeavors.

Accept Yourself and Open to More Visibility

For business owners, showing up on social media is a delicate dance between the need for consistent presence with the authenticity of their personal brand. Many of us are modest or may just not feel like sharing, especially if we are naturally the introspective type. The to-our-selves type. If this is you, hanging out in the studio working on your creation with just the Divine as your witness is the perfect way to share your world...

There are moments when we yearn to share and bask in the glory of our life's accomplishments with the cherished community of family and friends surrounding us. We desire to illuminate our inner world, allowing others to be inspired by our radiance. In order to make a meaningful contribution to this world, it becomes imperative for us to rise and flourish, becoming the beacon of light that leads and guides others. By embracing our role as a leader, we can share our unique gifts and illuminate the path for those who seek inspiration and growth.

As personal brand entrepreneurs, artists, mentors, authors, or inspirational leaders, we get the personal development "muscle" to show up again and again and share our learned wisdom and shine the light. We "get" to do that Facebook post or LIVE or Insta video to continuously contribute content back into the world.

It keeps us on our toes and expands us as not only business owners but as people on the spiritual path.

But what is that magic ingredient that keeps sourcing this?

Well, there are many. And it comes from that which is sourcing you.

Though there may be many moments when we are at total peace never being seen or heard except in the beautiful interior realm of the spirit, we are quietly encouraged to unfold into new spaces to radiate in the world. There is an overarching desire within our souls to touch that which is the truth for our highest path. And, while we do this work, persevering and continuing to show up and shine, something to watch for is how we perceive sides of the coin.

It isn't always that simple...

On the flipside of the coin there exists a part of us that finds solace in invisibility, yearning to retreat into the depths of the inner realms. This aspect is often projected onto us by the external world, labeling it as humility or modesty. While it is important to honor our need for introspection and introspective moments, it is equally vital to recognize the potential for self-limitation that can arise from excessive hiding. By finding a balance between visibility and retreat, we can navigate the world with authenticity, embracing both our inner depths and our capacity to shine brightly when the time is right.

However, there is great confusion around these things which can often go in the direction of self-deprecation. Yes, you can be a humble being in this world, and still shine the light in big ways. Part of that path is being seen in the world so that your message gets shared in bigger ways.

The other side of the coin stands in self-value that is free from egotism and narcissism.

It is up to us to inquire within ourselves how we are honoring and loving ourselves to be seen or not to be seen. To share, or not to share.

This all stems in the perception of how you relate to others seeing you.

Have you been told not to be too brilliant and beautiful? Have you been told to not be too bold, or others may not like you? You might fail?

There are many voices and projections of others that have told you to play small. But you weren't created to be small – you are here to be magnificent as an expression of your Maker.

Sometimes flashy is the sparkle of the sunlight on the ocean, or the velvety glitter inside a magenta rose. Neither knows modesty versus vanity. They just allow for their own beauty to *be* as a part of the Divine's creation.

We are all beautiful and all important.

You have what it takes to be successful, wealthy, happy and to create your own reality with every single thought.

You are worthy of greatness... not because of what you do, but simply because of who you are! The value you bring is who you are!

Allow your gift to compel you to share it. Remember, you succeed by helping others so you get to show up every day and have the power to do amazing things.

You are the creator of your life. Your reality. The life of your dreams.

You can be confident and inspired, and so much of this fuels your desire to show up, serve, and be visible.

Loving and accepting yourself is key to your visibility.

When you know nothing holds you back because you know you have something special to offer, you know you have what it takes, and are unstoppable to getting your purpose in the world, you are magnetic.

The world needs you to risk being in the spotlight. The world needs you to make it your calling to get your message out to the world.

So. It's time to break free from the chains you or others have put upon you around staying invisible.

Projections and judgments can turn into false core beliefs and shame. Often a parent, or another authority, tells us to dim it down early in life and the negative voice gets into our subconscious as our own voice and it slows us down...

Who were they to tell you to stop being bright?

Did they not realize you are here to be amazing?

Why would we even be influenced by another's ideas in the first place?

Let go of the need for acceptance. Not everyone will accept you anyway... and it doesn't matter − those who need you will soar when you soar.

Again, the value you bring is who you are.

You get to accept yourself, and know you're a child of the Divine.

It's time to turn back up your light and shine on.

And on and on...

And receive in avalanches of abundance that you may keep giving.

I want to encourage you to simply begin.

Your Path Through the Fourth Gateway

In the process of cultivating heart-centered connections in your visibility, it's deeply important to extend loving compassion towards yourself... first. Practicing self-compassion allows you to nurture your own well-being and authenticity, which in turn enhances your ability to connect with others.

Here are a few insights to integrate loving compassion towards yourself in this process as it radiates love into your visibility practices.

Cultivate a sense of self-acceptance by embracing your strengths, vulnerabilities, and imperfections. Recognize that you are a work in progress, and it's okay to have moments of self-doubt or make mistakes. Treat yourself with kindness and understanding, just as you would treat a dear friend. Embracing self-acceptance frees you from unrealistic expectations and allows you to show up authentically in your online visibility.

Engage actively with your audience by responding to comments, messages, and inquiries. Show appreciation for their support and contributions and make an effort to make meaningful conversations and connections as you seek feedback and listen to their input. When you engage with your audience genuinely, you create a sense of community and connection which of course leads to building your business and brand.

Emotional intelligence is the ability to become aware of and understand your emotions and those of others. It allows you to navigate emotions effectively and respond empathetically. Cultivate emotional intelligence by developing self-awareness, managing emotions, and empathizing with others. Practice emotional intelligence in your online interactions, considering the emotions and perspectives of your audience. This leads to deeper connections and more meaningful engagements.

Create a safe and inclusive online environment where everyone feels welcomed and valued. Respect diversity and encourage open dialogue. Create guidelines and boundaries to ensure a positive and respectful space for interactions. When you establish a safe and inclusive space, you go deeper with connections based on trust and respect.

Make self-care a priority when it comes to your online presence. Nurture your physical, mental, and emotional well-being by engaging in activities that bring you joy, rejuvenation, and balance. Set boundaries to protect your energy and create space for self-reflection and self-care practices. When you prioritize self-care, you show up as your best self, ready to connect authentically with your audience and even look more radiant on video if you do that.

Prioritize inner self-valued alignment, and focus on it by aligning your actions with your values and intentions. Listen to your intuition, honor your inner voice, and make decisions that feel aligned with your authentic self so radiate a sense of luminous love, attracting genuine connections with your audience.

Holy Hot Visibility Soul Action:

Mirror work is a self-love practice to begin to see yourself with new loving eyes. When I first did it I was struck by the realization that I was seeing into my soul. I felt as if I was reaching into my inner child that longed to be seen again, as well as reaching back into lifetimes.

Look at yourself, honor yourself. As you gaze into your reflection, you send yourself loving, self-affirming words and even take up a conversation like you are speaking with your most beloved friend. You are connecting with yourself in a profound way to become a more self-aware and confident human being. When you align with your inner power and integrate the pieces of you that need loving, you will accept yourself and your appearance as you are, heal shame that keeps you stuck, and show up in all the ways you must to fully express yourself and live your dreams.

Simply grab a handheld mirror or sit in front of a mirror at eye level and make eye contact with yourself. The key is keeping that eye contact as you send yourself love. Work through the cobwebs of comfortability or intimacy as you connect with YOU. Say things that are delicious such as "I AM..." affirmations. If emotions come up, it's okay. Keep loving yourself through those too. Also grab my free gift in this book, The 7 Holy Hot Gateway Prinicples pdf download at **HelloLucinda.com/freegift.**

4th Gateway Journal Prompts

1. Think about moments when you've felt disconnected and distant, from the people you want to reach. How can you approach this situation with empathy and sincerity to build a connection with your audience through your marketing and personal brand?

2. Dive, into the idea of being centered around compassion and understanding in your marketing endeavors. How can you incorporate empathy, kindness and genuineness into your brands messaging, visuals and interactions to establish a bond with the audience you desire?

3. Take some time to consider your values and how they align with what your ideal audience wants and needs. How can you effectively communicate these shared values in your marketing materials to foster a sense of connection and resonance?

4. Acknowledge the importance of actively listening to and comprehending the concerns, difficulties, and dreams of your audience. How can you integrate this understanding into your marketing strategies in order to address their needs and offer solutions?

5. Reflect on the power of being genuine when it comes to establishing a connection rooted in compassion. How can you authentically present yourself in your marketing efforts by sharing experiences and vulnerabilities that resonate with your audience?

GATEWAY 5:

SELF EXPRESSION

From Reserved to Expressed

Voice and Authenticity

"If you want to find your own voice, you are going to have to start to use it.
And if you want that voice of yours to carry your truth, your unique being into the world, then slowly and silently let yourself open to the language of your heart, gently wrapping your voice around it, letting your tongue, snake-like, inhabit your knowing. Seeking the nectar and fire of your truth. Forming spoken spells, spellings, words of your knowing, your truth.
Let them form like fiery butterflies, landing in other beings' hearts, into the earth and on to the wind to be planted and grown within this world, and within you." — *Brigit Anna McNeil*

The other day, while I was walking my labradoodle and listening to a throwback playlist, Celine Dion's voice came through my earbuds. It brought me right back to one of my first voice activations of being witnessed by people I didn't know.

When I was just shy of fifteen, I chose to do the seemingly unthinkable for a semi-shy lass: sing two songs for my solo recital, "Close to You (Why Do Birds Suddenly Appear)" by The Carpenters and "Where Does My Heart Beat Now?" by Celine Dion.

Now, if you know these songs, you know they're polar opposites – one is coy and demure and about birds suddenly appearing, seemingly from the anxious vice-grip of infatuation; the other is a booming powerhouse of broken-heartedness after losing love.

Yes, I'm a romantic. And though I didn't realize it until I was much older, I chose two songs to match the two aspects of my personality: the side that wants to be shy and invisible while questioning the birds' proximities (Karen Carpenter), and that embodiment of thunder, lightning rainbows and redemption (Celine).

I was shy and I belted it out anyway.

Somehow, by choosing Celine's as the second song, I was able to embody her power and really opened up. It's like I wanted to pay homage to the beauty of her love ballad and the epic emotion it imbued.

In that moment, I was channeling her and thus became a star. The room was empty and my voice was activated. I probably didn't hit every note perfectly, yet I felt alive and embodied. My inner performer was free as a bird, sailing in song over wide valleys.

When we open our mouths to sing or to speak, it takes this vibration from the realm of the unformed and moves it from within to without. The energy from your initial breath is cyclical and permeates your lungs, flowing through the second and third chakras, which are associated with creativity and showing respect for oneself and others. Rather than merely exhaling, pushing the air past the fourth and fifth chakras where the heart chakra and the center of will power and intention is housed, singing engages both the heart and mind.

The whole journey of the vibration activates the third eye and opens the prism door of the crown chakra before sending this vibration into the world.

It's soul alchemy! This can support you in harmonizing your frequency with the world and with the Divine as a purification of emotion, even if we are not fully aware of what we are singing. The power of the voice and music together are powerful tools to bring forward creation.

Whether you consider yourself talented or not, your voice is your birthright to belt out with song. It is life and vibrancy and yours to enjoy, no matter if it's taking it to the stage, in quiet meditation, or singing in the shower with your shampoo bottle as your mic.

One aspect of being visible is being heard. Even if you are hearing the medicine of your own soul.

Have you ever felt like you have something important to say, but you just can't get the words out? Or maybe you're afraid to speak up because you're worried about what other people will think. Whether it's in your business or in your personal life, learning how to use your voice is a powerful tool that can help you create the life and business you want.

Your voice is an essential part of who you are. It's unique to you and it's a powerful tool that can help you create the life and business you want. When you use your voice, you are able to share your story, your ideas, and your message with the world. When you don't use your voice, you miss out on opportunities to connect with others, to make a difference, and to build the life and business you want.

How to Rip that Tape Off Your Mouth & Activate Your Voice

If you're ready to start using your voice, here are a few things you can do:

1. **Speak your truth.** Tell your story. Share your message with the world. When you're authentic and vulnerable, people will be drawn to you and your message.

2. **Take risks.** Don't be afraid to put yourself out there or to try something new. The more risks you take, the more confident you'll become in using your voice.

3. **Practice, practice, practice!** The more you use your voice, the easier it will become. So find opportunities to practice speaking up, whether it's in a meeting at work or in a conversation with a friend.

4. **Use affirmative statements.** When you make declarations such as "I AM..." or "I CAN..." you are affirming your power and ability to create change. These statements will help empower and motivate you to use your voice.

5. **Be persistent.** Don't give up if someone doesn't listen or if they don't understand what you're saying right away. Keep speaking up and sharing your message until it's heard loud and clear!

Interesting how sometimes we can feel so shy or simply modest. We keep secret the parts of our soul and elements of God's creation to be shared in only the most intimate and selective ways. (I'm the type who keeps her clothes ON at the hot springs.)

Yet other times we take it off, metaphorically and literally, and others can like what they see or not; it matters not to us anymore.

The bigger picture is the focus, the meaning behind the content, not all the little details.

I was asked by a colleague and former design client to be photographed for the cover of BellaMia, a wonderful women's empowerment magazine, with much of my breast exposed representing Mary Magdalene as an archetype of being all-women.

Wow, was that a moment of visibility for me!

And I really thought nothing big of it... I didn't even feel exposed, it just seemed natural. It was an honor to represent Magdalene and working women and mothers, and to be a part of a great magazine. And it felt holy in my element and love of motherhood.

It was just as when I fell in love with my breasts (overshare for a teaching moment) after becoming a mother and experiencing their purpose in nourishing life. What these bodies can do are amazing!

Just the same, when we step up for a higher purpose, know our real why, and realize we are here to make a contribution, we can move beyond that feeling of being exposed in fear of being rejected by the world.

Allowing ourselves to rip the metaphorical tape off our mouths and express our voices and values is one of the first great steps in truly allowing our visibility to shine.

As female entrepreneurs, we often feel like we need to "have it all together" in order to be successful. We think that we can't show any vulnerability or "weakness," so we put on a brave face and power through – even when things get tough. But what happens when we internalize our struggles and keep them to ourselves? Well, eventually they come out one way or another.

Bottom line: when we try to bottle up our emotions, it only makes things worse. So how do we rip that tape off and start expressing ourselves in a healthy way?

Below are three tips that have helped me in my own journey of self-expression:

1. Set boundaries with your family and friends. It's important to have people in our lives who love and support us unconditionally. However, that doesn't mean that we need to share everything with them – especially when it comes to business. When you're first starting out, it's common to want to tell your loved ones everything in an effort to gain their approval or get their input. But, more often than not, this ends up causing more harm than good. They may not understand the challenges you're facing or the decisions you need to make, and they may give you unsolicited (and often unhelpful) advice that derails you from your path completely.

2. Find a therapist or coach (or both!). As female entrepreneurs, we often wear many hats – leader, manager, employee, friend, daughter, sister, mother...the list goes on. And while there's nothing wrong with being a jack-of-all-trades, it can be difficult to manage everything by ourselves without burning out. This is where having someone to talk to can be incredibly helpful. A therapist can provide you with a safe space to process your emotions and work through whatever is holding you back. A coach helps you focus on your goals and is a valuable investment in yourself.

3. Join (or start) a supportive community. One of the best ways to feel heard and understood is by surrounding yourself with people who get it – people who are going through the same challenges and victories as you are. These people can provide invaluable support, accountability, and encouragement throughout your entrepreneurial journey. If you don't already have a community like this in your life, consider starting one!

There are many online groups filled with amazing women who would love to connect with you.

It's time for us to start expressing ourselves – for the sake of our businesses and our sanity! By setting boundaries with our loved ones, finding a therapist or coach, and joining a supportive community, we can begin to peel back the layers and reveal our authentic selves.

You likely have many voices inside of you vying for visibility and expression. It can be difficult to know how to be seen and heard in the world when you're an introvert or empath.

Here are some ways you can play with being fully expressed and seen as a multi-passionate spiritual woman entrepreneur.

- **Share your story.** Don't be afraid to share your journey with others, even if it's not perfect. Your story is unique and it can inspire others to blaze the way in their own path.

- **Keep getting visible.** Make sure you are seen and heard in the places that matter to you. This could mean speaking up at meetings, networking events, or online.

- **Find your power.** Claim your power as a woman and use it to create the change you want to see in the world. You have a unique perspective and gifts to offer, so don't be afraid to share them with others.

As women, we are often socialized to downplay our successes, hide our light, and be modest. We are taught that it's not "ladylike" to brag or toot our own horn. We are told that we should be more concerned with others' opinions of us than our own. All of this can lead to us feeling ashamed of who we are and what we have to offer the world.

But what if we were to express the truth of ourselves, unapologetically and without shame?

What if we allowed our light to shine bright for all to see?

Here are three ways to naturally to shine:

1. Be proud of your accomplishments.

One way to start expressing the truth of yourself is to be proud of your accomplishments. So often we downplay our successes because we don't want to come across as bragging or conceited. But why not give yourself credit where credit is due? The next time you achieve something, take a moment to acknowledge it – and don't be afraid to share it with others. When you start celebrating your successes, you'll find that others will too.

2. Don't compare yourself to others.

Another way to express the truth of yourself is to avoid comparing yourself to others. We live in a world that is constantly comparing us – our looks, our accomplishments, our possessions. It can be easy to get caught up in this comparison game and lose sight of our own unique gifts and talents. Instead of comparing yourself to others, focus on mastering your own skills and becoming the highest version of yourself that you can be.

3. Be soulful and authentic.

The final way to express the truth of yourself is to simply be authentic. Be true to who you are, even if it means straying from the mainstream or deviating from what others expect of you. Live your life on your own terms and don't apologize for being exactly who you are meant to be. When you are authentic, people will respect you – and you'll respect yourself too.

These are just a few empowering ways through which women can unapologetically express their true selves, free from the burden of shame. It is high time for us to embrace a sense of appreciation in our achievements, release the habit of comparing ourselves to others, and fully embody our authentic selves. The world is in deep need of more women who boldly step into their own personal power, expressing their unique gifts and perspectives.

When we do so, we become unstoppable, unabashed, unashamed.

We just ARE.

When you know your deeper purpose to expose and release all excuses that have held you back, you shine with something that does not need to be named or labeled, but instead as simple wholesome authentic truth.

Glamour Meets God – Integration for the Multi-Impassioned

Every day you'll find me wearing my Birkenstocks. Not long ago you may have found me sashaying down Hollywood Boulevard in gold sparkling high heels.

The first big business investment for my business was on the upper end of 10k for a brand coach who made promises of getting us seen, known, and heard basically by embodying the rockstar vibe, a more performative and pushing approach that wasn't even true to my brand archetypes or essence. It was actually a trend in the early to mid 2000s in the online space and I would watch women following the trend, even though I could perceive it wasn't on-brand for them.

Heels, double set of fake eyelashes, and big sequenced gowns was a different and new direction for me, were not exactly the totality of my authentic nature. On one hand, it was fun and it felt a little like playing dress up like a child, but eventually I had to sort this journey out in my personal brand journey.

While this was a fun exercise that gave me much to ponder on, I quickly realized stilettos and pink prom dresses were not exactly the totality of my authentic nature. I'm the girl that grew up in the Pacific Northwest in her two pairs of Birkenstocks, one with covered toes for winter, and the other a pair of sandals for the three months out of the year it didn't rain. It was humble, unassuming, caring-for-the-environment kind of belief system.

Sometimes wearing neon and big bold style can be a way shower to help us embody a part of confidence in our psyche and serve as a helpful way to step onto the visibility journey, yet it can also bring about moments of shame as we realize it might not fully reflect our authentic essence and then we endeavor to rewild our brand to get back to a truer version of our expression, not influenced from external sources.

It's crucial to remember that there's no judgment here; it's about embracing the cycles of visibility and invisibility that we experience. These cycles can also manifest in our style, wardrobe choices, and color preferences, becoming integral parts of our self-expression.

When I moved to Santa Barbara County, I was in a wee bit of culture shock when I noticed so many of the women donned their designer heels with their designer jeans. And it's true, when there are so many international restaurants, posh cafes, art galleries, beach to mountains, and the whole movie star vibe, it's easy to fall into a little bit of a shoe fetish. Within weeks, I had more than a dozen pairs, and then that soon doubled. Luckily, I eventually was able to chill that out and home in on a variety of colorful sandals and quality shoes for my feet and I just accepted I liked a few more shoes.

Back to the midst of the high-end business program, I had more than a couple pairs of fancy heels. Golden sparkly ones, black ones with red soles, black and gold metallic with a stripe of green velvet, blue suede heels, and so on. It's what every entrepreneur girl boss should have in her closet, right? I was experimenting with what "California girl" should look and feel like, and living not far north of the home of the Hollywood stars, I was being influenced by the branding of American culture itself.

When attending an event in the heart of Hollywood, with the back door to the conference room offering a view of the iconic sign through the Pantages Theater and other tall buildings that tried to touch the sky, I took a break to walk up and get an almond milk mocha latte with half the amount of syrup pumps at the cafe on the corner. Inside, I was still the tree-kissing, Birk-wearing, Oregon Earth-Mama gal with the occasionally seasonal hairy armpits. And, I had my golden-auburn ombre locks in beachy curls, red lips on, with a tight teal cocktail dress and donning my gold heels with matching statement earrings.

And I did get the heads turned.

While this version of me wasn't one I wasn't accustomed to, I realized the value of what the business coach was saying. Dress like a certain type of goddess superstar and get noticed in your star power. After all, American, and particularly Hollywood and movie culture, shows us women that it's glamour that is what fuels our power, value, and deservingness.

I noticed all the parts of me that judged those with money and flaunting it in Southern California. And while that was true, and at times a bit ostentatious, I got on the journey of wanting to have quality and beautiful things that in the past I would have shoved aside as unnecessary. It all became part of my journey to discover the integrated parts of myself.

This approach would not be viable, in the run as I would ultimately learn to fully embrace my own love, joy and inner beauty as my authentic path.

Weaving together multiple passions has been part of the journey as it has been for so many of my multidimensional branding clients.

It can feel like an ongoing wrestling match of being the soul in the flesh...

We are like a diamond, sparkling with a multitude of passions.

It's a lot about self-expression.

You get to be how you need to be at various cycles, seasons and stages of the path.

You don't have to leave behind your inner mystic or your glamourous self; you don't have to feel like a sellout if you embrace it. This is how the holy-hot thing came to be. Let the contrast of your inner hippy-healer and outer glamour goddess create appeal, even as you allow the wrestling match to just be.

Allowing my artist-self, writer-self AND my career as a branding mentor to be seen and shine has been the most scary' but integrating experience. I continue to learn about these aspects of myself and, even as I write to you, I am learning and sharing what I need to know.

Holy Hot Visibility is about embracing ALL of ourselves and allowing ALL to be visible, first to ourselves and then to others. That includes our sensual, exotic passionate sexuality (as we've discussed, some of us chose to keep this more to ourselves than others), our desires, and our messy messes!

Makeup, as part of the "beauty standard," is another trigger for so many. If you feel a disconnect if I, or another, wears makeup or wants to apply a filter, let this be an inquiry for you. You can activate the depth you desire within yourself, rather than feeling judgmental about the way someone is expressing themselves. It doesn't necessarily mean they are inauthentic or dishonest. People can have many different reasons for doing what they do.

What feels the most poignant is to move beyond the oppression in society that has women perfectionizing ourselves to pieces.

They tell us to remove body hair, shave ourselves everywhere, wax ourselves, bleach parts, tighten things, remove things, color other things, get rid of flaws and stretch marks and scars, tighten our belly and fatten our lips, have ever-perky boobs and behind, be ourselves and be natural all at the same time... and not try too hard or look overdone because that's not attractive either.

We are told to wear makeup, conceal, contour, highlight and prime. Line things, fill things, lengthen lashes and bronze, blush and beyond. Our hair is too long or too short or too frizzy or too dyed or too gray.

We aren't supposed to age but to stay youthful; old isn't beautiful.

We are told to be pure and to not be a "slut" or sleep around. Not to have sex with too many men but have some fun too. We are supposed to be a sex goddess and also be pure and innocent.

We can't talk too loud or too much or take up too much space or be too intense or intimidating. We have to sit, stand and poise with presence. We can't be bossy, bitchy, or a diva. We can't be too emotional, too crazy, too passive; we can't cry or swear too much.

We are supposed to please and over-give to the point of burnout. Make your man happy. Be a good wife, keep him happy, cook his dinner, take his last name and become the "Mrs." of his last name.

And if that all tickles you, so be it. But I challenge you to erase and transmute the programing to find what makes you feel good.

I love cooking my husband dinner (most nights) and right now, I've let my silvers grow out, though I may choose to henna my hair. Either way, it's my decision, despite being told to "leave it!" by some and "You're too young to be turning gray" by others.

So if you find someone projecting their judgments on whether you are glam or natural, take some deep breaths and consider it an invitation for another to have their own mini transformation about learning about themselves and come back to you!

Realign with your inner truth and ground in your inner knowing.

What about our little neurotic ways? Our tortured inner artists and our ability to multitask in too many directions?

How do we moderate the parts of ourselves that are on the path of learning and have vulnerability to be woven into the overall brand story too?

These things too, the flaws, the foibles and falls, can be woven in as part of our learnings and teachings as we gain more perspective on them.

Here's to recognizing it's always about being visible to ourselves and the rest is kind of a reflection that goes out into the world... as much as we desire to share.

I recently ordered a pair of gold Birkenstocks since I love the way the warm light energizes and adorns my feet and I also want to feel rooted, not I'm going to fall off a pair of miniature stilts created by a king to make himself appear larger.

And whether you chose to wear Birks or heels, the sashay is where it's at. You get to own your strut and choose to step into your inner authority as a leader and expert of the wisdom you've gained just as you are.

Your Path Through the Fifth Gateway

Expressing your authentic voice and style is a powerful tool for effective communication and genuine connection in your online visibility. When you communicate with authenticity, you create a space for meaningful interactions, build trust with your audience, and convey your unique message with clarity and impact.

Here are a few practices to help you express your authentic voice in your online visibility.

Recognize that your voice and perspective are valuable. Embrace your unique experiences, insights, and opinions as they contribute to the richness of your online presence. Trust in your own voice and have the confidence to share your thoughts and ideas openly. Your authenticity and genuine expression will resonate with your audience, attracting those who resonate with your unique perspective.

Effective communication is key to conveying your message and building connections. Laser in on your communication skills by practicing deep listening, developing clarity in your expression, and using language that resonates with your audience. Strive for clarity, simplicity, and authenticity in your written and spoken communication. As you refine your communication skills, you'll be able to express your authentic voice more effectively and engage your audience in a meaningful way.

Share your story! Your personal story holds immense power and serves as a powerful vehicle for authentic expression. Share your journey, experiences, and challenges that have shaped you and your work. Connect with your audience through storytelling, allowing them to relate to your experiences and form deeper connections. By sharing your story authentically, you create a sense of vulnerability and human connection, fostering a genuine and lasting relationship with your audience.

Continue to practice active authenticity by aligning your online presence with your true self. Be consistent in your messaging, live in alignment with your values, and show up as an authentic representation of who you are. When you embody authenticity, your audience can feel it, and they are more likely to connect with you on a deeper level.

By embracing and expressing your authentic voice, you invite genuine connection, build trust, and leave a lasting impact on your audience. Through effective communication, storytelling, and active authenticity, you can establish an online presence that connects with your audience, fosters meaningful connections, and amplifies the power of your message. Remember, your authentic voice is your superpower, so embrace it, share it, and let it guide your online visibility journey.

5th Gateway Journal Prompts

1. *Think about moments when you have felt a bit reserved or hesitant to express yourself. How can you. Strengthen your throat chakra to overcome these limitations and embrace self expression in your personal branding and visibility efforts?*

2. *Dive, into the concept of discovering your voice within your journey. How can you. Amplify your voice and perspective to stand out in your industry? How can you use your voice to inspire educate or entertain your audience?*

3. *Take a moment to reflect on any fears or insecurities that might be holding you back from expressing yourself in regards to your branding and visibility. How can you let go of these fears and step into the power of being an authentic communicator?*

4. *Consider the significance of clarity in your branding and visibility endeavors. How can you refine your messaging to ensure it is clear concise and aligned with both your brands values and goals? How can you efficiently communicate your message to reach your ideal audience?*

5. *Explore the power of storytelling as a means for self expression in efforts. How can you craft stories that captivate your audience while conveying the essence of your brand? How can storytelling help create a connection, with, well as build trust among those who follow you?*

INSIGHT

From Unseen to Seeing

Intuition, Imagination, Perception, Wisdom

"Work in the invisible world at least as much as you do in the visible..." — Rumi

As spiritual entrepreneurs and spiritual human beings, we know a whole lot about the invisible etheric realms. Intuition is of course part of all we do as we honor that path of inner understanding, discerning, and knowing. In our branding and business, these speak not just with the eyes, but the soul. Our inner knowledge is here to create depth and connection with those who align with our branding.

I have called myself a visionary artist and also an intuitive web designer as so much of my inner seeing for my clients comes from an almost psychic knowing of their essence after I feel into them a bit. Some of it is my perception of who they are and their qualities, innate gifts, and energy. When you feel seen and expressed in your visual branding, your photos, and everything comes together as YOU, it's easier to show up naturally and share your website because it feels like an extension of you. Its evocation, emotion, and energy are aligned with you.

Through photography my clients have learned to "see themselves," or those loveable, worthy aspects, for the first time. It's as if my camera's "lens of love" reflects the same beautiful potential and gifts I have seen in them. This is how you should feel when looking at your photographs. If you don't, have them taken again or take a deeper look at the emotions they are bringing up for you and do the work around that.

Allow Your Intuition to Be Your Guiding Light

I've played a game with myself over the years as I've moved through self-doubt issues and whether my intuition was guiding my choices or I was in my head and being guided by my ego.

As a sensitive being, I have struggled with a certain level of trauma, as most people do. These can include anything from the loss of a loved one, divorce, being bullied or abused, having an accident, or any other shocking undesirable event.

Part of the visibility journey involves a profound healing that extends to various levels of our being, including the development and trust in our spiritual gifts. Along the way, we encounter residue from worldly experiences, some of which may have been traumatic, leaving imprints in our bodies, minds, hearts, and psyches. Recognizing that these imprints are intertwined with how we regulated our nervous systems during those moments, we can engage in healing practices that nurture self-trust, cultivate resilience, and embrace our authentic visibility.

As we heal from our trauma, whatever that looks like, we learn to trust ourselves to discern between what feels safe (as discussed in Gateway 1) and what is controlling our life with anxiety.

Sometimes I like to play with my intuition by picking out what color I want to wear each day. I stand at my closet and take a breath, feel my feet, and allow myself to receive the colors my eyes gaze at. You can ask out loud or within yourself, "What is the color or clothing choice that will help me align with the essence I desire to be expressed in today?" You can change the words slightly to suit what can be supportive to you.)Keep slowly breathing, and feeling into what feels alive and delightful.

You will gain answers from a freer part of yourself that lives outside of your mind. You can ask questions with the simple example of your outfit and get deeper as you go on to use it for social media posts, course creations, business decisions and more.

Ask if it comes from love or from fear. Is it intuition or anxiety?

Keep listening, trusting the answers, and keep gleaning more wisdom when you mind might be overriding the intuitive guidance and then keep coming back to your innate knowledge.

The more you practice this, the more you will begin to trust yourself and go with these answers.

You can practice this in self-care, the types of clients you choose to take on, the ways you evolve, and so on.

Watch when FOMO (fear of missing out) arises and the impulsive desire to respond and leap from this space of lack. Kindly tell it to bow down and share with that part of you that it isn't correct or truth, and this place comes from fear or trauma, and no thank you.

Your inner wisdom is not conducted or rooted in fear. It doesn't feel like it's an emergency when you get grounded guidance aligned in your intuition.

Your inner wisdom speaks in a kind, clear, and often quiet confidence. This is what I intend for you – to keep practicing and strengthening, which will support your ability to get more visible in all aspects as you continue to build trust and boundaries around your decisions. This happens organically when you continually respond from this rooted space within.

You won't as easily fall into the trap of shame and threats to pull you don't that path of scarcity, urgency and anxiety when you are tapped into your truth.

Reinforce this important work with healthy self-talk so you embed it in your cells more deeply. Tell your inner child (some call this the ego or little voice that can feel scared), that you will be there for them. *"Sweetheart, I am here for you, and I will listen to your requests and make the best decisions for us."* That is the wise intuitive whole self holding space for other potentially fragmented parts.

When we act from a grounded place of intuition, we become attuned and deeply connected to our mind, heart, body, and soul. This integration encompasses all aspects of ourselves, allowing us to be fully present and responsive to our evolving needs and desires as they arise.

In the Holy Hot Visibility course , we will explore more aspects of ourselves with exercises and tools to increase our power and renew our inner intuition in holistic ways that will empower you in life and your business.

Seeing Ourselves with Self-Expression

"Women express themselves differently than men. They communicate with more feeling, more intuition, and more heart. They also have an innate knowing that they are connected to something much larger than themselves." – Michaela Boehm

Women tend to communicate from a place of feeling and intuition, while men tend to communicate from a place of logic and reasoning. This is not to say that women are illogical or that men are insensitive, but rather that each gender has its own way of understanding and relating to the world.

For example, a woman might express herself by sharing her feelings about a situation while a man is more likely to state the facts of what happened. A woman is also more likely than a man to express her emotions through body language and facial expressions. This difference in communication styles can often lead to misunderstandings between genders.

Women have a unique ability to express themselves in a way that is authentic and deeply felt. When we do, we open up the possibility for magic to enter our lives in wonderful and unexpected ways. Unfortunately, this same ability can also lead to shame if we feel like we are not living up to our own potential or the expectations of others.

The truth is, there is no need to feel ashamed of who you are or what you are capable of. You are perfect just as you are. And when you express the truth of who you are, you open up the possibility for magic to enter your life in wonderful and unexpected ways.

For example, a woman might feel ashamed of her abilities if she does not meet the expectations of her family or friends. She might also feel ashamed if she compares herself to other women and feels like she does not measure up. The key is to remember that there is no need to feel ashamed of who you are or what you are capable of. As those of us who watched Mister Rogers will recall, his takeaway message was always that we are perfect *just as we are.*

Your Path Through the Sixth Gateway

Awakening intuition is a transformative journey that allows you to attune with your inner wisdom and harness it with regard to your online visibility. Intuition is a powerful tool that can guide you in making aligned decisions, connecting with your audience on a deeper level, and infusing authenticity into your online presence.

Here are a few ways to help you awaken and cultivate your intuition in your online visibility:

1. Developing a strong connection with your intuition begins with deepening your self-awareness. Take the time to reflect on your thoughts, emotions, and inner knowing. Tune in to your body's sensations and subtle energy and pay attention to the signals and nudges that arise within you. By becoming more aware of your inner landscape, you can start to discern your intuition from other external influences and choose ways of being that are truly soul-aligned.

2. Cultivate presence as an essential treasure for accessing your intuition. Engage in your favorite spiritual practices to quiet the mind and create space for intuitive insights to emerge and unfurl. By anchoring yourself in the present moment, you open yourself up to receiving intuitive guidance and inspiration for your online visibility to lead your next inspired acts.

3. Trust your gut, baby. As counterintuitive as it might sound, intuition often speaks to us through gut feelings or a sense of inner knowing. Learn to trust these intuitive nudges and honor them in your decision-making process when faced with choices or opportunities in your visibility. Trust that your intuition has a deep understanding of what is in alignment with your authentic self and your highest good, when you need to rest, and when you need to make the whole place shimmer.

4. Create moments of solitude and silence – by the sea, in the forest, or under the stars somewhere. This allows you to connect with your inner wisdom and intuition and connect with the regenerative power of nature. Set aside dedicated time to unplug from distractions, both online and offline. In these quiet moments, you can listen to the glorious whispers of your intuition and receive guidance that may not be accessible in the noise of everyday life and social media. Embrace this Still, Small Voice as a pathway to deeper self-discovery and your intuitive awakening like the peony in the early summer sunshine.

Take it a step farther and designate dedicated time for sacred solitude retreats where you can retreat into a nourishing shushed space. Create a sacred environment that promotes relaxation, such as your favorite beeswax candles, playing ambient music, or surrounding yourself with aromatherapy and anointing yourself. During this retreat, fully disconnect from the digital world and allow yourself to recharge so you can truly engage in activities that bring you joyful peace, such as reading spiritual books, journaling, stretching or meditation, or simply spending time in creation. These self-led retreats provide an opportunity for deep introspection, self-care, and replenishment of your energy reserves and rewild your brand.

If you identify as an introvert or highly sensitive individual, it's essential to regularly clear and protect your energy body. Engage in clearing practices that resonate with you, such as smudging with sage or Palo Santo, practicing sound healing, or engaging in visualization techniques to release any stagnant or negative energy. For me, prayer from the heart and navigating through the emotions to be lifted by the Divine is what works. Ask for what isn't yours to be returned, and for what is yours to be returned to you in the heart of your sacred space. By regularly clearing and protecting your energy field and coming back to yourself, you create a harmonious and supportive space for your intuitive connection and personal growth.

Bottom line, intuition is your inner Yoda in making decisions for your online visibility. As you cultivate your intuition, practice incorporating it into your decision-making process and engage in intuitive exercises, such as visualizations or intuitive journaling or free flow art pages to tap into your intuitive insights and allow them to inform and lead strategy... not the other way around. Trust that your intuition holds wisdom that can lead you towards authentic and aligned actions and allow yourself to honor what comes through in these deep wellsprings of guidance.

Awakening your intuition in your online visibility journey is a profound way to infuse authenticity, alignment, and soulful connection into your presence. By deepening self-awareness, cultivating mindfulness, trusting your gut feelings, seeking solitude, and practicing intuitive decision-making, you can harness the power of your intuition to create a meaningful and impactful online presence.

Embrace your intuitive gifts, and let them guide you on the path of shining brighter with less fear.

6th Gateway Journal Prompts

1. *Think back, to moments when you felt unnoticed or undervalued in your efforts to build your brand and increase your visibility. How can you tap into your instincts, imagination and understanding to gain insights and develop a perspective that allows you to be recognized and appreciated?*

2. *Delve into the concept of intuition and its role in establishing a brand. How can you trust your instincts to guide the direction and decision making of your brand? How can you integrate practices into your strategy for a genuine and aligned presence?*

3. *Ponder the influence of imagination in shaping your brand and visibility. How can you utilize your abilities to envision an impactful brand identity? How can you tap into your imagination to innovate and stand out in your field?*

4. *Contemplate the significance of perception when building a brand. How can you be mindful of how others perceive both yourself and your brand? How can you consciously shape the image and messaging of your brand to cultivate a perception among your audience?*

5. *Reflect on the wisdom gained from experiences + expertise. How can you leverage this knowledge to establish yourself as an authority within your industry? How can you better communicate your knowledge and establish credibility with your audience?*

Part Three

Becoming

SPIRITUALLY EMPOWERED

From Unknowing to Known

Divine Connection, Beauty, Self-Belonging

*"Oh God, help me to believe the truth about myself,
no matter how beautiful it is."*
— *Ameera Beth*

Reverence for Beauty... a Feminine Pathway to God

The seventh chakra, or crown chakra, connects the virtue of beauty and the spiritual realm. It helps you to understand who you are beyond your physical self as a spiritual being having this human experience.

Beauty is an integral part of our intuitive knowing. It serves as a guiding force that is deeply personal and unique to each individual. Defining beauty becomes an enigma, as its essence defies a singular definition and remains subjective to our individual experiences. It also fluctuates and invites contemplation and exploration throughout the various chapters of our lives. Beauty is a virtue that comes straight from our Divine creator. It is far more than a thing of appearance, but a perception of the presence among us.

All we have to do is look for beauty, and there she is all around us at any moment. Beauty speaks to us softly and can also shout her glory from the rooftops. Beauty is available for us to gaze in awestruck wonder at her splendor. It's easy to adore and want to be in a relationship with her as she seduces our senses.

Beauty's obviousness can be in a gorgeous man or woman or subtle like the spiced colors of an autumn leaf as it spirals downward to its earthy resting place. We can find it in the infinite wonders of nature, in the myriad glories of colors, in the scintillations of the stars and the hues of light in sunrises and sunsets.

Beauty will forever inspire my works of art, photography, and designs.

Beauty is the ultimate alchemist as she shapeshifts from one thing to another, in various scents, flavors, colors and textures. She lives among the impoverished and also the rich and she knows no bounds... we can find her everywhere.

I've been told I'm a Beauty-Seer. I have been told I'm a channel of Divine Beauty. And I have been told I am "beautiful", which tends to have all sorts of responses as a human being and our associations around it. I've experienced evolving levels of healing in my issues around beauty over the course of my life.

Around age thirteen, I was new to my middle school and was quite hesitant in coming forward in outgoingness. Let's just say I was even more introverted and shy back then.

I remember being called a "bitch" by a couple other girls. I later found out because I was both quiet and "pretty" that they assumed I was a bitch. I didn't realize until much later that I had created a small thorn of trauma around having beauty and would strive to be seen as funny or intelligent... and at times work to undermine my beauty to not intimidate other girls or women and, well, be perceived as a bitch. I also found myself very offended when other women were called the b-word.

In high school, my plump, outspoken friend called me "skinny bitch" as her affectionate pet name for me. In later reflection, that was definitely a way to make herself somehow feel better about herself, but again, being thin, tall and pretty didn't feel so safe...

Just out of high school I turned "hippie," wearing neutrals and no makeup, one pair of Birks and baggie clothing. I wanted to be seen as spiritual and was afraid of being next to anything material or worldly. I worked at a bead shop and began learning about a myriad of spiritual paths what I later learned fell under the umbrella of "New Age." I played with crystals, talked to the moon, and got back to the earth. I wanted to be an Earth Child and walk as far as possible into the forest, away from the mornings when I spent an hour doing my hair and makeup before school to live up to the comparison others had made of me to Cindy Crawford. Big hair, eyeliner, and carefully lined red lips, baby. That was all exhausting, but I sure got a lot of attention. However, not all of it was actually wanted so I always associated getting fancy with attention from guys I needed to be careful not to end up in a room alone with.

This was another tick in my beauty-wounding.

Over the years I played with going invisible and being more visible through makeup choices and clothing colors. I've watched big cycles even for a few years at a time with these patterns. I look back and see the reasons why I did what I did, almost to balance the cycle before so the pendulum could eventually find its equilibrium point.

I've dressed to please mates, communities, and cultures.

I look back with loving eyes at the inner people-pleaser, always looking for approval, and know it to be part of my trauma response to stay safe, to not stand out too much in the wrong way, and to avoid getting burned at the stake.

I have called my women out in their personal brand photos for criticizing and crucifying their God-given beauty and instead shake what their mama gave them at any stage of life.

And it's not easy. Accepting the natural signs of aging can sometimes be accompanied by a grieving process, especially when we witness the emergence of silver hairs or the appearance of wrinkles on our necks that we may prefer to hide under a turtle neck. It is reminiscent of the observations we made while witnessing our mothers and grandmothers gracefully age into their own seasons of life, much like the trees displaying the beauty of their changing seasons. Just as the trees acknowledge and honor the transition and inherent beauty of each season, we too can learn to appreciate and celebrate the unique beauty that comes with the passage of time.

When, for Goddess' sake, will we accept the extra weight that hormones and changes of life bring? When will we fully embrace the crow's feet and claim them truly as a symbol of beauty, of all the radiant smiles we have graced others and the world with? *When?*

I am grateful to mentor others to stand in their own version of beauty unapologetically.

And I endeavor to do the same for myself in the ups and downs of my weight and the valleys of life where I look at a Facebook memory photo from just around the corner called the Past and wonder, where did that gal go?

Well, she's right smack there in the middle of my body and my soul. And the maiden will always dance in each of us.

Just a bit ago, as I was writing this book, I paused to adoringly witness my sleeping three-year-old's breathing, his arms still wrapped around his bear from tuck-in time. Each of us has that immaculate untainted innocence sparkling in the quiet reaches of our psyche, the places before society and others' judgments took hold.

If we can accept beauty that resides way beyond what meets the eye, the beauty of the soul and love the fullness of that, our cup is brimming over with what deeply matters.

What a high honor to be a channel for the flow of beauty into the world in its many forms, as my life path thus far is all about it – be it making paintings that express the beauty of the Divine feminine, photoshoots to help women feel beautiful as the radiant light beings they are here to be, or creating beautiful websites for all my clients.

Beyond my livelihood, I seek beauty in others as the children of the Divine we each are. It is beyond the limiting human flaws we only perceive from a small space.

Beauty becomes a practice all day long in the realm of color as I'm completely in love with the realm of the emanations of the rainbow. Color has always been an undulating expression of this prismatic realm we call life, and I count my blessings – and the gift of sight to be one of the most blessed – for this amazing planet we dwell in, in addition to the visionary spiritual experiences we can perceive on the inner plane.

But of course, beauty is far beyond what we see.

Beauty is an expression beyond words or measurements of what many associate with the Divine feminine and the expression of Her. In my feminine experience as a human, it has been the main doorway on my path to divinity.

Beauty furls open the petals of the heart and activates our love to see more clearly into truth.

It is an expression that we can sense in the ecstatic blessing of life when we are in full reverence of it. Beauty becomes a spiritual principle that is essential for living a pleasure-filled life expressed from the heart.

Beauty can be the sweet tears behind joy or the shimmer in the eyes that reflect the purity of being a Divine being in a human body. Beauty carries the beholder beyond its source and straight towards the merging of God.

To take it deeper, beauty is often perceived in the heartbreak, longing, or the precious sweetness of life. It can be in both the pleasure and pathos of the human experience, and can be a bridge for the duality in the experience.

Sometimes we can experience so much beauty and heart expansion it almost overwhelms the heart, brimming with the mystery of this amazing life and beyond. We can offer this beauty up in devotion to the Divine, to surrender our little piece in the vast experience of the infinite that is within us. This Divine expression knows that which is beyond humanness, beyond any limited thinking, and showers upon us in the most glorious rains... cleansing and purifying us anew each day.

Beauty is the breath of love, and this love merges into timelessness which is the truest fulfillment of that beyond which we can ever see with the eye, paint into form, or inhale deeply from the rose.

This isn't about the puffed-up ego, like: *"Hey look at me 'cause I'm looking so good in this photo,"* or *"First, lemme take a selfie,"* (because of vanity and narcissism). It often is quite the REVERSE journey for most of us to move through seeing and accepting ourselves, to look back at one's own soul in the shell of this body and then share it with others as a journey of self-love as we practice greater non-judgment as human beings and honor ourselves.

This ocean runs deep, and when you begin to swim in it more, it means honoring your soul as an expression of the Divine.

And then expressing ourselves and honoring the Divine within as the presence of God, the I AM, right here within our souls. It means having so much reverence for this presence in our lives at every moment that we stand in our fullest power and fulfillment as an abundant daughter or son of the Light. A lavish expression of I AM THAT, I AM.

So swim deeply and then rise from the ocean. Come expose yourself to the breezes and sunlight. Step upon your own stage -- I want to hear you say it with your heart: "HERE, I AM."

In beauty, we walk the path to taste and discover the Infinite.

Beauty Exercise #1

Spend the day looking for what you find beautiful. Really bring your intention into focus. I am certain you will start to sense things, feel things, and see things that uplift your soul and help you feel that connection and oneness with our Creator.

I imagine you will also discover these things of beauty to have been present in your life more than you appreciated before, so this will enhance your connection to gratitude and appreciation... which makes everything more beautiful!

Beauty Exercise #2

Create something beautiful. This will be unique to you, or another's experience. Then play with inquiry... what does this experience do for you? Did you have a spiritual experience from this? Journal for a few minutes about beauty and your experience to anchor it in a new way, and how it flows into your life as part of your spiritual path to the Divine.

We Belong to Ourselves

Most black sheep of the family become the healers to break the shadow of the generations to start their own lineage. Here's to shifting the curses of guilt, fear, shame, and lack of understanding.

When I was very young, I hung out with the cud-chewing four-leggeds.

My folks and other adults were enchanted that I was able to commune with these sheep that flocked to our pastures in the summers. I was able to get close enough where I could read their tags and with my freshly sharpened pencil I would inscribe their number on the illustrated tag of their ears.

I would sit for hours, like I did with my tree, at the edges of the pasture quietly observing their peaceful nature and reflecting upon mine.

They would keep watch on me, and I would gaze at them, looking into their eyes in search of some recognition of silent communication. I would wonder if and how they housed a soul.

There was a being-ness that I longed for even as a child, and I experienced the simplicity of just the existence of spending hours with their head to grass endeavoring to get enough during a day's grazing.

The individuals of the flock didn't judge me, and they seemed to listen to me as we stared into each other's eyes in the zone of quiet being and pure resolution. They, chewing on their cud, and me, with my developing frontal cortex, doing homosapien things like writing books, having human relations, and other activities requiring cognizant brain-firing.

We were a quiet constellation in the pastoral countryside of the Pacific Northwest. With my young mind, I noticed no one else desired to sit and meditate with the sheep. I was alone in my peering into the microscopic natural world of the ground level to witness the dew accumulating on gossamer that scintillated even in the foggiest of mornings. I was solitary in spying the tiny leafhoppers collecting their blade forts made with bug spittle. I was joyful in befriending the curious-eyed newts that dwelled among the grasses as I daydreamed about other worlds at fairy levels.

In this natural environment, I was at one. I knew I was part of the creation, just like the ewe, the newts, the spit bug, and the blade of grass.

There was no separateness. It was my inner world and outer world holistically merging in my moment. There was nothing else. I was totally invisible to the rest of the world, and fully witnessed by the world around me.

It was almost as if I could hear voices. In fact I did hear voices, which I knew intimately and adults called "imaginary friends." Retrospectively I consider these beings some of my guides that are likely still with me.

We are never truly alone...

The main being that visited me was a wise man with a silver beard, long flowing hair, and a magical cane rustically carved out of wood. He was powerful and playful all at once, and emanated biblical essence like Moses himself. We even had a whole language that I would try and teach my sister the extraterrestrial-esque letters that in my adult life reminded me of paleo-Hebrew letters.

He was as real as day for me.

I would speak with him through my left wrist. Yet I communicated with him because I felt alone.

He and my Magic Maple Tree were my best friends, and the sheep and the many other creatures of the meadow were great companions as well.

I am sharing this with you because, while hiding in the pastures, I found my sense of belonging in the world.

I would come inside to be with my family and my place would shift perspective and there was a sense of labels and projections by other humans on to me, even my loving family. I felt a sense of judgment and often didn't feel safe to fully be myself. I later learned that I could be with them.

Often, I would feel like the odd ball. The black sheep. The misunderstood. I was more emotional, introspective, and imaginative than my sister and parents and often called "sensitive." Not that they didn't have great qualities, I seemed to be the one who saw worlds within worlds, and lived in this rich realm of color, artistry, expression, and wild possibilities.

The false belief of being separate isolates us from the rest of the flock. Yet in this, there is a great beauty to be found. We discover our uniqueness and learn to deepen our own sovereignty. We learn to find the Divine.

"Who you are is separate."

This false belief of being the black sheep creates a wound of isolation. The idea we are just innately separate is about as bizarre as having original sin... like just because we are born into the world there is something inherently wrong with us.

When you're perceiving that you're disconnected, something feels like it's not right...You want to just disappear into the woodwork. When you are cherished and respected, you feel recognized and often understood.

BEING YOU IS A SOURCE of contribution — it lights up your career and relationships.

When you are witnessed in that and received in that belonging, you are connected in love and respect for being who you are with others.

Unless we felt a part of something, we wouldn't think about belonging unless we felt like the black sheep. Things come to light when they need to come up and be transmuted and healed and therefore being integrated back into the Source and place from which we came, dwell, and are going.

Growing up, I perceived some of the feelings and ideas I had weren't cared about, appreciated, or respected. It wasn't intentional or malicious on my family's part, it was just a differentiation between belief systems or personality types.

As a child, I was often quite shy and would become paralyzed when speaking to people. There would be mornings when I couldn't decide which shoes to wear because I couldn't bear the idea of making the wrong choice. Even now, I acknowledge that I possess the quality of being a considerate decision-maker, and I've become increasingly aware of how my highly sensitive nature amplifies this trait.

I just wanted to dwell in the pasture with my animal friends and not have to worry about screwing up, upsetting others, or feeling their disapproval.

As I've mentioned, much of my life, I didn't feel like I fit in, except in spiritual communities perhaps because we were relating on a subject far greater than our little human flawed selves. After leaving an emotionally abusive relationship where I was completely isolated, I was taken under the wing of one of the woman elders at the meditation community I would live in for the next eight years. I remember sobbing while we sang songs together, realizing that there were people in the world that were loving, kind and considerate who felt like soul family.

I felt loved. I felt seen. I started to reconnect with my heart and others.

Years later, I fell in love with the mystical path of Judaism. When I converted, almost each time I shared about my conversion with another Jew, I was told I "was welcome to the tribe." As I deepened in the culture, every time I met someone Jewish they would feel like family and I sensed a warmth with the "other" as we instantly had a connection. Cultures form traditions and my Jewish life was filled with rituals connected to the phases of the moon and rooted in thousands of years of repetition of custom. We did it as a people, and I had experienced no other sense of belonging as I did within the structure and spirituality of a people and one of the oldest religions.

Belonging was about being with like-minded resonant people who are there for each other's love and respect deep soul connection.

In attuning to our blacksheep-ness, we find our uniqueness and develop our own self-expression. This is a gift when we are creating personal brands where we stand in our individuality that doesn't try to look or act like anyone else. This is where our unique essence comes forth and we don't have to think so much about competition because we aren't worried about differentiating ourselves because we are accepting our own differences.

We may think relationships feel false because we aren't able to connect. Sometimes we can think in order to have a place, we have to be different. That can serve us to a point but the source of this idea creates cracks to form. Because we all need to belong and have that feeling of oneness.

Your Path Through the Seventh Gateway

It is essential to recognize the transformative power of transcending limitations and connecting with Divine inspiration, your gateway to higher consciousness, allowing you to tap into your spiritual essence and align with your most brilliant self in the branding realm (and all of creation and life).

As we journey through the path of the Seventh Gateway, we find ourselves in a realm of transcendence, where we rise above limitations and tap into the infinite well of Divine inspiration and spiritual alignment like the dove taking flight on the light of dawn, reminding us of our interconnectedness with all beings and the world around us.

As we delve deeper into our online visibility journey, it becomes clear that true fulfillment and success come not from external validation or material gains alone, but from a deep sense of belonging with ourselves and our world. When we align our online presence with our spiritual essence, we tap into a profound source of inspiration that guides our actions and amplifies our lasting impact and desired legacy.

Transcending limitations in our online visibility means embracing the expansive nature of our being and recognizing that we are part of a greater cosmic dance that involves surrendering our ego-driven desires and allowing ourselves to be conduits for Divine guidance and wisdom.

When we align our intentions with the greater good and infuse our online presence with love and compassion, we become vessels for transformation and healing even in the online marketplace.

It is also essential to cultivate the practice of Divine surrender. This means letting go of the need to control every outcome and trusting in the flow of life and the digital world. Surrendering allows you to release resistance and align with the Divine plan that is unfolding for you.

It's about letting go of the urge to control or manipulate situations and, instead, permitting life to steer you towards the best manifestation of your online presence.

Surrender the need for control and allow yourself to be guided by spiritual alignment. Recognize that there is a higher purpose unfolding in your online visibility journey, and trust in the unfolding of Divine timing and synchronicity. Surrendering doesn't mean being passive; it means aligning your actions with the guidance received from your spiritual connection. Let go of the need to have all the answers and allow the universe to guide you toward the right opportunities, connections, and strategies for your online presence as you bask in the feminine receptivity part of doing business.

By embracing surrender, you unlock the door to receive the blessings and opportunities that are destined for you. Have confidence in the timeline of your journey towards online visibility, trusting that everything is progressing according to a Divine and perfect plan. It's crucial to remember that we are not aimlessly drifting like amoebas in the vastness of space; rather, we are active co-creators of our destinies. Therefore, taking inspired action is essential.

As we connect with the Divine in all these ways, we bring forth a unique energy that resonates with our audience on a soul level and our online presence becomes a source of upliftment and empowerment, offering a sacred space for connection and growth. We transcend the limitations of self-doubt, comparison, and fear, and instead, radiate a luminous energy that invites others to move forward on their own journey of self-discovery and expression.

In this shimmering space of deep belonging, we realize that our online visibility is not merely a platform for self-promotion or business growth but a channel for sharing our unique gifts and contributing to the collective consciousness. Our purpose becomes aligned with the greater unfolding of the Universe, and our online presence becomes a catalyst for positive change and meaningful connection that ripples beyond our simple humanity.

May we remember that transcending limitations and connecting with the Divine is an ongoing practice... it requires us to continually nurture our spiritual alignment and look within. By embracing our role as spiritual beings navigating our brands and businesses, we can bring forth a profound sense of purpose, authenticity, and belonging, allowing our online visibility to become a beacon of light in a world that yearns for truth, connection, and love.

This is the 7th Gateway of your Holy Hot Visibility.

7th Gateway Journal Prompts

1. Think back, to moments when you've felt a lack of trust or disconnected from your self in relation to branding and how you present yourself to the world. How can you develop a sense of strength that builds trust within yourself and in the way you showcase your brand?

2. Explore your beliefs and practices. How can you incorporate these beliefs into your branding and strategies for being visible? How can you infuse spirituality into your brand's messaging to connect with your audience?

3. Take some time to reflect on any experiences or negative encounters that might have contributed to feelings of distrust. How can you heal from these experiences. Let them go, fostering a sense of empowerment within your personal brand? How can you show up as an genuine presence for your audience?

4. Consider the significance of aligning your values with your brands mission. How can you ensure that your efforts in branding are harmonious with your principles and beliefs? In what ways can this alignment elevate the visibility and impact of your brand?

5. Reflect on how intuition plays a role in shaping your journey. How can you rely on intuition to guide decision making processes and steer the direction of your brand? What are effective ways to communicate this knowing and wisdom to connect with your audience?

PUTTING IT ALL TOGETHER

Bridging the Gateways

Allies for Your Brand Mission in the World

Throughout your Gateways journey, you have embarked on a transformative exploration of self-discovery, healing, and empowerment. Each chakra represents a unique aspect of your being and holds valuable insights and qualities that can greatly support your brand mission in the world. As you integrate and align these chakra allies, you unlock a powerful synergy that propels you forward in manifesting your purpose and making a meaningful impact.

The First Gateway, the center of the root chakra, with its focus on safety, security, and stability, provides the foundation upon which your brand stands. It helps you establish a solid and grounded presence, enabling you to navigate the online world with confidence and resilience. By addressing any fears or insecurities related to visibility, you create a sturdy platform from which your brand can flourish.

Moving up to the Second Gateway, you are embracing your creativity and authentic self-expression. This chakra ignites the fire within, infusing your brand with passion, originality, and magnetic energy. It empowers you to connect deeply with your audience, resonating with their desires and needs through authentic storytelling and engaging content. Your brand becomes a vibrant tapestry of creativity and emotional connection.

The Third Gateway empowers you to harness personal power and confident leadership. It encourages you to step into your authentic voice and claim your unique value in the online space. As you embrace your personal authority and take courageous action, your brand becomes a beacon of inspiration and influence, radiating confidence and attracting the right opportunities and collaborations.

With the Fourth Gateway, the heart, you cultivate heart-centered connection and authentic relationships. This chakra reminds you to lead with love, compassion, and empathy in all your interactions. Your brand becomes a vehicle for creating a positive impact, spreading kindness and fostering a sense of community. By nurturing genuine connections, you establish a loyal following that resonates deeply with your brand's values and mission.

Moving to the Fifth Gateway, at the throat chakra, you embrace authentic communication and expression. This space empowers you to share your voice, ideas, and expertise with clarity and authenticity. Your brand becomes a powerful platform for sharing your message, inspiring others, and sparking meaningful conversations. You engage in open and honest dialogue, amplifying your influence and establishing yourself as a thought leader in your niche.

The Sixth Gateway, also known as your "sixth sense" or the third eye, opens the gateway to intuition, inner wisdom, and spiritual alignment. It guides you in making aligned decisions, recognizing opportunities, and tapping into your higher guidance. By trusting your intuition, you infuse your brand with a sense of purpose and Divine inspiration, attracting opportunities and aligning with your soul's mission.

Finally, the Seventh Gateway, your crown chakra, connects you with Divine inspiration and transcendent wisdom. It reminds you of your interconnectedness with the universe and aligns your brand mission with a higher purpose. Your brand becomes a channel for sharing light and love with the world, uplifting others, and making the positive difference you crave.

As you bring the journey of the Gateways together as allies for your brand mission in the world, you create a holistic and harmonious expression of your authentic self. You embody the qualities and energies of each chakra, infusing your brand with a unique and soulful essence.

Your online visibility becomes a sacred space for transformation, inspiration, and connection, serving as a catalyst for personal and collective growth.

Embrace the power of the Gateways as allies for your brand mission. In my Holy Hot Visibility course, we integrate their teachings, qualities, and energies; allow them to guide and support you as you navigate the digital landscape, spreading your message, making a meaningful impact, and unlocking a profound synergy that propels you forward in manifesting your purpose and shining brighter with less fear. I invite you to join me on this journey if you are ready to go deeper.

What's The Difference Between Vision, Mission, and Purpose?

So you want to make a difference in the world? *I feel you, sister.* So do most spiritual women entrepreneurs.

You know that your sacred gifts can create positive impact and change the lives of others. By now, you've likely dreamed of monetizing your skills and doing something meaningful in the world.

But how do you turn these dreams into reality? How do you become an entrepreneur who creates positive impact for yourself and your community?

The first step is to set an intention which will connect you to purpose. Before you start any business, it's essential that you get clear on why you want to be an entrepreneur and what kind of impact you want to make in the world. Visualize yourself in the future, when your business is successful, and imagine what impact it has made. This will help keep you motivated as you work towards achieving this goal.

The next step is to stay connected with your values and passion. It's important to remember why you started this journey in the first place – to share your sacred gifts with others. Keep a journal or make a vision board so that every day, when things get tough, you can look back at what inspired you in the beginning.

Lastly, don't forget to practice self-care while striving toward success. As a spiritual entrepreneur, it's crucial that you care for yourself in body, mind and spirit. Make sure to set aside some time each day for meditation or yoga or whatever activity helps ground and center yourself so that when obstacles arise (which they inevitably will) you are ready to face them with grace and composure.

As a spiritual entrepreneur, it's essential that you stay connected with your values and have an unwavering dedication to making a positive impact for those around you by sharing your sacred gifts with them. By setting an intention for success, staying connected with your values and passions, and taking care of yourself along the way, you can create real transformation in the world through entrepreneurship and manifest your dreams into reality.

You want your work to matter. And you want to build a legacy that lasts. But what does that actually mean? How do you translate your big dreams into tangible goals?

Let's take this further.

The first step is to define your vision, mission, and purpose and how your visibility plays in. These three concepts are often confused, but they're actually quite different, and I like to think of them as your three sacred gems to share in the world.

Vision aligns you with your goal (aspirational). This is the gem of your aspiration. Your Vision is what you want to create in the world. It's your long-term view of the future and it guides your decision-making in the present.

Mission empowers how you will accomplish it (tactile). Done well (being visible!), it will inspire and motivate you each day, as it will your audience. Your Mission is your WHY. It's the reason you do what you do. It's the change you want to see in the world.

Purpose keeps you centered on why you exist (soulful). Your Purpose is your North Star. It's the thing that gives your life meaning and makes you feel fulfilled.

Most people have a hard time articulating their Vision, Mission, and Purpose because they haven't taken the time to think about it deeply enough. But if you can get clear on these three things, everything else will fall into place.

Here's a way to express your vision;

Take a moment to imagine the kind of world you'd like to be part of, in the five, ten or twenty years. What changes do you aspire to see within yourself your business, your community and the world as a whole?

Now consider what steps you can take today to bring yourself closer to that vision. It's alright if you don't have all the answers now. Your vision will naturally develop over time as you gain clarity and experience.

The key is simply getting started.

And here's how you can articulate your mission;

again reflect on the change you wish to see in the world. Why is this change important? What difference will it make once it becomes a reality?

Now ask yourself what actions you can take today that will help advance that mission. Your mission should ignite excitement and inspiration within you. It should go beyond gains. Aim for a lasting impact that extends far beyond your own lifetime.

Lastly lets explore articulating your purpose;

Many individuals falsely believe that their purpose must be something, like "saving the world." However this isn't necessarily true.Your goal could be as simple, as making others feel acknowledged and understood or offering a product or service that simplifies peoples lives.

Your purpose is personal to you. Originates from an inner place. So ask yourself "What brings me joy? What ignites my passion? What gives me the sense of fulfillment?" Once you have the answers to these questions make it a daily practice to take action even if its something

I suggest starting with your purpose because it serves as the groundwork, for everything else.

And don't forget your Holy Hot Visibility — this is the golden thread of shining and being your sacred three gems in the world.

No matter what stage you're at in your journey as an entrepreneur, it's never too late (or too early) to get clear on your Vision, Mission, and Purpose. By taking some time to really think about these three gems, you can begin to build a legacy that lasts – a business that matters and makes a difference in the world that I know your heart desires.

The Pathway of Creation: Embracing Your Prosperous Brand

Your brand is so much more than words or visuals. It is the treasure chest and the promise of what you are sharing with the world. This encompasses a lot of things; it's your vibes. It's your authenticity. It's you, showing up. It's like a story and it's an essence that's coming forward to someone. So this accompaniment encompasses a lot of things, but really at your core, your personal branding is like who you are showing up in your frequency.

When we come to this space, we are learning how to connect with the healing and all the work we have done on the journey with our souls, the Divine and our spiritual nature as we allow for it to integrate into our physical lives and embody it in our business and lives to use it for GOOD!

Now that we have traversed the dichotomy and integration of being Holy AND Hot, let's peek into their integration and the Pathway of Creation to create your brand and visibility.

The inner leads to the outer. The path of alchemy is one thing moving to another and sometimes back again.

What does the term "as above, so below" mean? It means things in the heavens above are the same down here on Earth. It suggests the universe reflects the inner self, with one level of reality mirroring another. The phrase comes from the Emerald Tablet, and is a key text in Hermeticism, stating *"That which is below is like that which is above, and that which is above is like that which is below."*

All of creation is inner connected and we don't have to put the Divine in a "place" anymore. We can know the idea of the macrocosm reflects the microcosm and the other way around.

This concept parallels with personal branding. Just as the phrase suggests that the universe is a reflection of the inner self, personal branding also begins with introspection and self-awareness. To establish a strong and authentic personal brand, we must first understand our core values, passions, strengths, and unique qualities. This inner exploration acts as the foundation upon which their external and online expression will be built.

Once individuals have a clear understanding of who they are and what they stand for, they can begin shaping their brand identity in the external world and online.

The process of personal branding involves carefully crafting the way we present ourselves to others. This includes defining a clear and consistent message, creating a visual identity, and curating a professional online presence through social media, websites, and other digital platforms. All these aspects should align with your inner values and aspirations, making the external representation a genuine reflection of your authentic self.

Just as the Emerald Tablet states, "That which is below is like that which is above, and that which is above is like that which is below," personal branding acknowledges the interconnectedness between the internal and external aspects of an individual.

A strong and well-developed personal brand is a harmonious union of who the person is at their core and how they are perceived by others in the world and create a powerful and congruent personal brand that resonates with others and reflects their true essence.

"As it is above, so it is below."

The Alchemical Pathway of Creation: Inner and Outer Branding

Invisible > Visible
Intangible > Tangible
Spirit > Matter
Visualization > Reality

The way I like to think of branding is in terms of vision to reality. We dream in the visualization and imagine its reality as we are stepping into the next version of our future self. We envision the business of our dreams and then we create it. We raise our self-worth and step into royal confidence. Become and we live our brand. The inner gets visible on the outer. We find our people, or our people find us, and we make an impact.

We bring our shadows into the light as we evolve and heal in an unlimited spiral of simultaneous ascension and rooting in worth.

We take the invisible to the visible. The inner chakra work transformed into wordly aligned influence.

We express the inner brand, the intangibles such as your essence, your vibes, your personality, your gifts, and blessings... who we are meets our future self and vision.

The inner becomes the outer, the tangibles such as your colors, your logo, your website, your signature offers, your photos, your styling.

This is the sum total of your prosperous brand expression. This is all your experience, personally and professionally, that has gotten you ready for something amazing. I teach my students in my mastermind how to craft their offers from the magic and sum total of all you've done and spin it into a lucrative, beautifully packaged brand.

There is no one else in the world like you and your unique soul's signature is ready to shine on the planet. Your inner Empress is your ally. With her, there is no competition — there is no one but you. You become magnetic and clients and opportunities seek you.

Community collaborations and referrals, when you are clear and authentically exuding your true self, people know who to refer you to sprout like a wellspring of potentiality.

You work smarter, not harder, your personal brand conveys your message so you don't have to work as hard.

You step into confidence! (You know what you're all about + how to share your message, babe.)

Get the confidence to be seen.

What is your grand vision? That thing that God has placed on your heart? That dharma to fulfill? And how does your message want to be delivered?

Do you want a book that touches the world? To speak from stages or sing it from the rooftops?

What does your future self have to tell you a few steps down the road?

Take some time connecting with your Future Self exploring the next steps.

Connect to Your Future Self Meditation

Connecting with your future self can be a powerful experience, one that can unlock answers to the questions you've been seeking.

The first step in connecting with your future self is creating a space of reflection and meditation. Spend some time alone and quiet, allowing yourself to relax into the present moment without any distractions or outside noise. Take several deep breaths and allow yourself to feel grounded as you open up to whatever comes next.

Get comfortable, close your eyes, and take a few more deep breaths. Visualize yourself looking one, five, or ten years into the future, seeing and feeling what it would be like if all your dreams came true.

Engage all five senses – what do you see, hear, taste, touch, or smell?

Picture yourself in this place of success – what are you doing? Who are you surrounded by? What does it feel like to live out these dreams?

Now that you have visualized yourself one, five, or ten years from now in this place of success, ask questions about how you got there. Imagine yourself talking to this version of you – ask her how she made it happen and what advice she would give you right now that could help guide your path toward making those same dreams come true? Allow yourself to really listen within for the answers before opening your eyes.

Connecting with your future self can provide insightful guidance on next steps in life while also inspiring hope for what lies ahead. When we tap into our own potential by creating space for reflection and visualization, we can gain clarity on our deepest desires and receive invaluable wisdom from ourselves. Allow this practice to become part of your weekly routine so that over time, these questions will become second nature as they guide you along the path towards achieving all that is possible.

Also deep dive in the gorgeous gift I've made for you, the 7 Holy Hot Visibility Principles download to refer to. You can find that in the free gift section at the back of the book.

When you have the fuel of your purpose, Your Prosperous Why, you can begin to let that spill into your brand story and marketing as you go.

How do you figure out your true life purpose?

Here are some insights and steps to help you navigate this process:

Step 1: Expanding exploration

Discover and explore what comes easy and natural to you. This is part of your brand statement above but let's go a little deeper. You can always add to your notes above.

We are all born with a meaningful purpose and deep passion we get to discover in life. Some of us know it at an early age, and many struggle to unfurl it over time popcorned with surprises and purposeful blessings. It's not something we have to invent, it's more of an inner archaeological dig to uncover its treasures. From the discovery, you can home in on specifics and expand your talents. Whatever you tap into, it should feel in the stream of your unique genius. That space that feels fun, alive, and when you do it time seems to dissipate.

I love to make art, write, create courses, pray to and teach about the angels, photograph people, bring out their essence in their brands, and strategize six-figure and beyond strategy for my clients. I share what the inspired muse within leads me, double checked by what makes sense.

Surround yourself with sources of inspiration, whether it's reading books, listening to podcasts, or connecting with mentors and like-minded individuals. Seek guidance from those who have been on a similar journey or have aligned their passion with their purpose. Learn from their experiences, insights, and challenges, and let their stories inspire and guide you along your own path.

These things come easy for me. Even the training, practicing, learning, and developing these talents felt grace-filled. What I mean is that creating your craft is required, but that should feel joyful as well. The joy is the juice in life purpose fruits, not arduous struggle or strain. If you're feeling the latter, you usually aren't yet in the realm of your hot Prosperous Why.

Step 2: Expressive Enjoyment

Expressing the purpose you were born with can be as simple as enjoying the virtues and qualities you most love to express. When we are in alignment with our true nature, we feel a sense of expressive enjoyment – an aliveness and joy that comes from being our authentic selves. This is the highest expression of who we are, and when we are living our purpose, we naturally exude these virtues. Take time to reflect on your interests, values, and the activities that bring you joy and fulfillment. Pay attention to what truly lights you up and ignites your passion. Engage in self-exploration practices such as journaling, meditation, or creative activities that connect with your inner desires and aspirations.

The world needs more people who are living their purpose and expressing their unique gifts, so ask yourself, "What is mine? What virtues and qualities do I most enjoy expressing?" It is time for you to step into your power and share your light with the world. The world needs YOU.

Allow yourself to be curious and explore different avenues that pique your interest. Follow the threads of curiosity and see where they lead you. Sometimes, your passion-aligned purpose may reveal itself through unexpected opportunities or experiences. Embrace new expressive experiences and be open to trying new things that resonate with your curiosity.

Expressive enjoyment is at the heart of why we are here and what we are here to do. When we identify and live our purpose, every day feels like an adventure where new possibilities await us. However, oftentimes we can get caught up in the mundane tasks of life and lose sight of what brings us joy. The key is to find ways to infuse moments of expressive enjoyment into our everyday lives, no matter how small. Maybe it's taking a different route to work and soaking in the scenery along the way, or listening to your favorite song on repeat as you cook dinner. When we make expressive enjoyment a priority, we not only feel more alive, but we also attract more of what we desire into our lives.

What are the virtues and qualities you most enjoy expressing?

Love? Joy? Appreciation?

How are a couple ways of expressing those qualities?

For example;

> *Inspiring and empowering others.*
> *I inspired others with bringing the light.*
> *Helping others who want to help people.*

Step 3: Craft your Living Vow (Mission Statement)

Take a few minutes and write out your vision of what the world would look and feel like if it were running ideally according to you. What is the highest vision where they are being and doing and having everything desired? Weave these elements into something you can speak with intention and keep by the side of your bed or wake up to as you refuel your fire each day for your Prosperous Why, why you're doing the work you're here to do.

My Hot Living Vow is, *"I am empowering, inspiring and uplifting others to become their highest version of themselves and live the most blessed life surrounded with beauty, abundance and purpose."*

Step 4: Let Divine Guidance Lead You

I have become more and more in awe of having my own guidance system to help get me from one place to where I want to go. It's like having a map that guides you when you feel lost.

Sometimes I reach out to be guided in prayer or meditation and listen until I get the next up in the queue, clue or sign.

You need to know where you are so you can get to the next place. So you will attune to the directions moving forward... where are you now and where is your destination?

Then you focus on where you are going. It's all about the pathway, the steps and listening to how to follow the inner guidance that is here for all of us.

Pray to the angels, the Divine to speak to you and show you the way. Intend for it, know it, trust it. Follow the map in discovering and rediscovering your purpose. I've included a bonus prayer at the back of the book, if you'd like an inspiration example.

Once you have gained clarity about your passion-aligned purpose, take inspired action to bring it to life. Section your goals in steps and create a road map for your journey. Start taking small, consistent steps toward your purpose, whether it's creating content, offering your services, or initiating meaningful projects. Trust in your intuition and take courageous steps forward, knowing that each action brings you closer to living your purpose fully.

To ground the idea of why your Prosperous Why is delicious as a human being; you can also identify the ways the fruits of the why materialize as worldly prosperity.

What are the other levels of your whys?

Financial independence for self and others?

To be able to travel?

To have more quality time with your family?

To get bodywork three times a week?

Donate to charity regularly?

Remember that the discovery and evolution of your passion-aligned purpose is not a destination but a lifelong journey. Embrace the process of growth, learning, and expansion as a natural part of the journey. Stay connected to your inner guidance, cultivate self-care practices, and allow yourself to find joy and fulfillment along the way. Celebrate your progress and embrace the lessons that come with the journey and trust in the unfolding of your path and stay connected to your inner spark as you create a meaningful and purposeful life aligned with your deepest passions.

IT'S YOUR TURN.

Okay, gorgeous. It's time to get out there and be visible. You have the magic you need to make a splash and get noticed in the ways that are aligned for you.

Remember these keys and hold them in your mind and heart as you step into the light of visibility:

1. **Believe in yourself.** The first step to being seen is believing that you have what it takes to be successful. When you radiate your birthright of confidence, people will take notice.

2. **Put yourself out there.** Don't be afraid to put yourself out there and be visible. The more you expose (it's not a bad word) yourself to the world, the more likely it is that people will take notice of you.

3. **Be unique, be you.** Be true to yourself and don't try to be someone you're not. When you stand out from the crowd, people will remember you.

4. **Keep learning.** Always keep learning and expanding your horizons. The more knowledgeable you are, the more you'll keep expanding and sharing.

5. **Stay passionate to your soul.** Pursue your soulful passions with gusto and let the world know what makes you tick. Beyond people being drawn to those who are passionate about what they do, you will remain true to yourself.

You have the opportunity to be heard, to be appreciated, and to be valued. This is the lifetime you can do it without the fear of persecution, woman.

Being visible doesn't mean that you're perfect, it just means that you're willing to show up and be seen. And when you do, people will take notice.

You will have the power to make a difference. You can inspire others with your story, your work, and your message. You can create opportunities for connection and collaboration. You never know who you'll meet or what kind of impact you'll have when you're out there being seen.

IN CLOSING

We've journeyed together through the vision. We've lit-up the inner transformation. Now you are becoming. That's right, Darling, you're ready for the game. It's time for your sacred stage.

It may not be a physical stage with the lights blaring on you and the audience so quiet as you could hear someone drop their program brochure or a baby babbling mama-mama-mama.

This is your moment when the dancers who are backstage, adorned in their glory as they await the music cue and spotlight, or actors on opening night who've spent countless hours memorizing lines over coffee, in the shower, and on the subway.

You don't need to rehearse your lines anymore. You've done that.

You don't need to think about placement, you've already envisioned that, you've practiced, and you know the dance of your soul.

I know you've got this because I've watched you. I know you've done this a million times. Yes, you may be nervous, but trust me, you've got this.

Remember Marianne, who took her stage, and how meeting her was a stretch for me at my level of visibility at the time? Now, through the four years it has taken me to complete this book, she's running again for the presidency of the United States of

America. Just as she has risen to her stage, you too have the power to step up to yours.

And, over these past four years, with the whirlwind of life events including three relocations (and about to be moving again to buying my first home), raising teenagers, welcoming a new son at 42, serving dozens of branding and website clients, making art, and living out my passions, I've completed this book and continued to grow in my life's work and visibility. During this journey, you've grown, too. It's time to set fire to your stage and be seen.

You've got this. You know what you're doing.

Lights, camera, action...

Step forth in all your blazing star-fire and the devotion to your soul purpose treasures. Now, I want to see you shine in *your* Holy Hot Visibility. Let the world see the radiant being you are.

You are ready. You are capable. You are seen. And most importantly, you are not alone on this journey. As you close this book, open your heart to the limitless possibilities that await when you step into your power and visibility. *This is your awakening call.*

So, what are you waiting for?

The world is ready for you. Let's get started...

Take Action

Free Gift For You

I have a special gift for you, dear reader—the Holy Hot Visibility Principles. These affirmations are incredible allies on your journey, uplifting your Holy Hot Visibility vibration. Get your complimentary PDF filled with the potent principles to empower and inspire your expansion. Download here: **HelloLucinda.com/freegift**

Holy Hot Online Visibility

Dive deeper and discover the power of your unique potential with my program designed for creative, spiritual entrepreneurs. This course will empower you to uplift your relationship with visibility, embrace your voice, transcend societal conditioning, and connect to your purpose. Get ready to step into your potential and shine like never before. Learn more: **HelloLucinda.com/hhov**

Prosperity Branding

Elevate your brand with the exclusive year-long program or opt for my VIP days for highly-efficient website and branding services. We delve into your vision, values, and unique offerings to create a brand that's authentically you. We also offer custom website, photography, and branding packages. By the end, you'll have a potent brand, an impressive website, a powerful marketing strategy, and the confidence to shine in the spotlight. *Ready to shine?* Apply at **WorkWithLucinda.com**

A Living Visibility Vow

So swim deeply and then rise from the ocean.
Come expose yourself to the zephyr and the dawn's light caress.
You came into this life for something greater.

Claim your rightful space, inhabit your wildest dreams, and
express yourself with unbridled love, leaving behind all inhibitions.
Deep within, you feel the spark that ignites your soul's soil. Listen
closely to the winds of a higher purpose, conspiring to liberate you,
granting you the courage to embrace authenticity and audacity.

You are coming out of hiding.
This is your moment to shed the cloak of concealment and step
into the magnetic wholeness that is your birthright. It's time to
abandon the habit of playing small to spare others' comfort and
instead, courageously embrace your innate power.

As you heal the scars of shame, judgment, and never feeling
"enough," remember that you possess a magical essence that
effortlessly flows through you. Look in the mirror, and with a
loving kiss to your reflection, acknowledge and activate
this enchantment.

Embrace yourself fully as a woman, and let your dance upon the earth reflect the wild, glorious creature you are, perfectly aligned with God's creation. You are not just a part of it; you are the embodiment of a unique rose, transmitting your essence to the world.

Now is the time to reclaim your embodied, beautiful expression and bring it authentically into your business and life. The world yearns for and requires the unadulterated YOU, raw and real, boldly stepping into your power. Leave excuses at the door, for they have no place here.

Express yourself completely, in the way you need and as you are meant to. As you fill your own cup, you become a beacon of light for yourself and those around you. Arrive as your authentic self, and generously share your gifts with the world.

Stand upon the stage of your own life and declare resolutely, "HERE, I AM."
Know this deep in your being: you are enough.
You have always been enough.

Bonus Prayer

Holy One, Creator of all things, Divine Consciousness, Source of Blessings,

I call upon You, Infinite Compassion, for humanity and for the balance of righteousness, truth, beauty, and grace within me. I seek your guidance and blessings for courage, strength, and protection in all our endeavors.

Divine One, I offer my gratitude for this day, this beautiful creation, and this life. I cherish each moment as a gift, a canvas for learning, wisdom, and transformation. I embrace this day's flow, ready to manifest my purpose and draw from the depths of my being.

Help me open my heart, mind, body, and soul at this very instant. Enable me to keep my heart receptive to your peace, prosperity, and love, illuminating my path. Assist me in revealing the boundless depths of your unconditional love and the riches flowing through my existence.

You are the giver of all gifts, Divine One. I pray for the awakening of abundance that constantly surrounds me. May my crown chakra and soul's aperture expand to receive your limitless bounty, prosperity, and love.

I am open to your flow, your currency, your river of life. Please help me be a vessel for your complete and limitless prosperity and love in all that I think, say, and do. Bless me with the abundance of your heavens and your Earth, guiding me into your light, love, and bountiful prosperity.

I celebrate life as your gift, now and forever. Thank you for your endless blessings. I am an abundant expression of your manifest riches. I am your child, here to create heaven on Earth in this lifetime.

Divine Creator, I know you forgive me always, and I am grateful for your continuous guidance. I forgive myself for past moments of darkness within my soul, both intentional and unintentional. I also forgive myself for any self-inflicted harm.

I release all false mental patterns and emotions that were not aligned with my highest good in the past. I humbly ask for forgiveness from those I have unintentionally hurt.

I understand that my life reflects my consciousness, and I accept full responsibility for my actions. I release victim consciousness and all forms of negativity.

Today, I repent and humbly ask for Divine mercy and compassion. May your radiant presence and healing light cleanse me of unforgiveness, bitterness, self-judgment, and judgment of others. I release all forms of negativity and vow to do better with humility and reverence for all life.

I forgive and release everyone, asking them to also forgive and release me. I humbly request forgiveness, healing, and wholeness.

I commit to honoring all life, treating all beings with compassion, staying connected to my heart, and aligning with my conscience. I choose to be courageous, righteous, and serve.

I renounce negativity, hopelessness, pessimism, and resignation. I release victim consciousness, poverty consciousness, scarcity consciousness, group consciousness, and powerlessness. I embrace leadership, power, success, impact, and prosperity.

I let go of blaming, complaining, worrying, judging, and chaos. I cultivate self-discipline, equanimity, non-reactivity, non-attachment, humility, integrity, righteousness, and courage.

I am here to serve, contribute, and reflect Light into this world. I am a powerful bearer of the Light. I embrace Life with willingness, trust, gratitude, enthusiasm, and the courage to be fully seen in my expression.

Please release me from the need for approval, value, or appreciation. Keep me free from false projections and judgments of others. Help me release ego attachments and the need for fame, shining from my depth.

May I serve, contribute, exude abundance, and create a lasting legacy, just as the sun shines endlessly upon me. I share generously, embracing visibility, and offer my gifts to the world as I shine brighter with less fear.

Acknowledgments

On my life's wild adventure, I've been luckier than a unicorn in a four-leaf clover field to have amazing friends, mentors, and supporters who've been a spark in my personal growth fires. They've not only helped me navigate life's obstacles but have also been my life coaches and spirit guides all rolled into one.

Thank you to God and the angels for hearing all my prayers and helping me transmute my shadows back into the light many, many times as I've allowed this thing I call visibility to expand and blossom.

Thanks to my Divine support team, I've turned life's lemons into lemonade so refreshing that even Beyoncé would want a tall drink. Their guidance has been the secret sauce to keeping my mind sharp and my spirit soaring higher than a caffienated eagle. Through the integration of these fresh outlooks and newfound skills, I've gained the strength to live authentically.

I would like to thank Merav Richter for holding my hand with structure, coaching as well as inspiration for this book along the journey of our work together. Your heart, beauty, and timeless wisdom are limitless.

Megan Walrod for your sparks of inspiration and the Boot Camp where some of this work was birthed years ago, I value and cherish our colleague connection and friendship!

Shanda Trofe for your encouragement and grounded hand-holding and support provided a sense of security, and your extensive publishing expertise made this journey feel smooth.

Thank you to my editors Dana Micheli for your perseverance and craftsmanship which have been outstanding.

I want to extend my heartfelt appreciation to the incredible mentors who've played different yet equally vital roles in my journey, your guidance has been the GPS on my entrepreneurial journey, guiding me through uncharted territory.

A special thank you to Sunny Dawn Johnson, who not only entrusted me with creating art for my first oracle deck but also provided unwavering support during some challenging moments.

Thank you to my beautiful friends who believed in me and especially Onyay with your loving and almost-daily audio voice notes and your big belief in this body of work.

To my husband, you've been my steadfast companion through the valleys and mountains, patiently tolerating my ever-evolving creative and sometimes crazy ideas. Your support is a little daily miracle. And our son, a most magical blessing of all.

Last but not least, a nod to my parents for being the artist and the writer, shaping me into the unique hybrid of you both. For my two adult sons that inspire me to be the best mom I can be at any given moment, and for my brilliant beautiful sister's loving support; couldn't imagine life without you! Your constant support and nurturing influence have been my guiding stars on this incredible journey.

About Lucinda Rae

Lucinda Rae is an award-winning artist and internationally acclaimed prosperity brand strategist. She specializes in enhancing your online and offline offerings through design and strategy, drawing abundance and audience with natural magnetism, captivating visual branding, and celebrity-quality photographs.

Delivering graphic design, visual identity creation, branding, online marketing and website development for over twenty years, Lucinda has created over 300 brand identities for corporate and creative entrepreneurs, iconic strong feminine leaders, and has captured thousands of stunning images and graphics.

In her photography, artwork, and graphic design, Lucinda's magic is empowering your unique journey to be authentically expressed as the magnificence that you are as you bring more beauty, inspiration, and purpose into life for your global community and legacy.

Lucinda is the founder and owner of Prosperity Branding, her boutique brand agency that has helped entrepreneurs business owners at all stages develop magnetic personal brands, best-selling book covers, and stunning powerful websites to support and build the business of their dreams.

From startups to multi-million dollar creators, Lucinda's personal brand clients include business and life coaches, luminary leaders, authors, creatives, therapists, spiritual teachers and more.

She has created several bodies of art including a multi-award winning children's book, the *I Am Prosperous Deck* and *The Multidimensional Oracle* with Internationally Acclaimed Psychic Sunny Dawn Johnston, and she offers unique courses for soulful creators that combine marketing and branding with manifestation and intuition.

Lucinda's expertise combined with her intuitive and visionary artistry and ability to see into her client's greatest potential make her branding work unique that it supports her clients in stepping into who they are becoming way beyond just having a new website, book cover or logo. Her unique Prosperity Branding system is holistic, strategic and fulfilling while utilizing brand archetypes as the cornerstone of her work to create iconic brands for luminary leaders to uplevel their life and business.

To learn more about Lucinda, visit **HelloLucinda.com** and be sure and check out the resources page for free goodies or go directly to **ProsperityBranding.com** for branding and website services. If you want to peruse her available art: **LucindaRaeArt.com**

www.ingramcontent.com/pod-product-compliance
Lightning Source LLC
Chambersburg PA
CBHW071347210326
41597CB00015B/1568